A CATHOLIC VISION

A CATHOLIC VISION

Stephen Happel and David Tracy

FORTRESS PRESS   PHILADELPHIA

Library of Congress Cataloging in Publication Data

Happel, Stephen, 1944–
    A Catholic vision.

    1. Catholic Church—Doctrinal and controversial works—
Catholic authors—Addresses, essays, lectures.
    2. Catholic Church—History—Addresses, essays, lectures.
    I. Tracy, David. II. Title.
BX1755.H26 1984   282   83–5687
ISBN 0–8006–1719–3 (pbk.)

K110E83   Printed in the United States of America   1-1719

CONTENTS

FOREWORD

A *Catholic Vision* by Father Stephen Happel and Father David Tracy is the second in the triad of books that Fortress Press is presenting of succinct, scholarly expositions of three major American religious faiths: Judaism, Catholicism, and Protestantism. It was preceded by Rabbi Howard R. Greenstein's *Judaism—An Eternal Covenant,* and the series will be completed by *Protestantism—Its Modern Meaning,* now being written by an eminent churchman.

As the editor of these books I am grateful to both Happel and Tracy, for they have opened wholly new worlds to me, a non-Catholic, and have made me acutely aware not only of the spiritual, cultural, and intellectual legacies bequeathed to us over nineteen centuries by this major sector of Christendom, but also of the gigantic efforts now under way by the Church of Pope John Paul II to face the problems of today's world.

At the same time I am impressed by three other aspects of *A Catholic Vision:* first, the eloquent yet restrained affirmation of Catholicism, its venerated traditions and contemporary messages; second, the solemn but muted note of acknowledgment of an indebtedness to Judaism, mother faith of Christianity, coupled with an implicit reproach to their fellow Catholics, both past and present, for their persecution of the Jewish people; and third, the confession that Protestantism in its infinitely varied forms is an inevitable outgrowth of a Catholicism that had allowed its intellectual strength to wane and its spiritual powers to diminish. This treatment is truly "catholic" in the full sense of an oft-misunderstood word, for its catholicity lies in its universal, all-embracing outlook.

A Catholic Vision reminds us of the richness of the Catholic Tradition, the wealth of wisdom it bespeaks, and its hospitable outreach to other Traditions, especially Judaism and Protestantism, in appreciation of their distinctive truths. For example, the treatment of the Protestant Reformation is high-minded and objective, and Catholicism is not portrayed as blameless or without fault. Also, the

Counter-Reformation is presented in a clear, dispassionate, unbiased fashion. Finally, the authors critically note some of the present-day trends within Catholicism and are clear and candid in their comments on the contemporary Catholic scene.

As Fathers Happel and Tracy say so aptly in their preface, their experiences as priests and teachers have also been "catholic," for the juxtaposition of their rural and urban posts in these past years deepen their insights and embody their faith.

I am happy to have had a part in the inception, the formation, and the development of this distinguished work. I, a Protestant, have grown in mind and spirit with A *Catholic Vision*.

I am indebted to Fathers Happel and Tracy for their gift of A *Catholic Vision*, a new and fresh perception of our ecumenical faith.

June 1983   Carl Hermann Voss

Carl Hermann Voss is Ecumenical Scholar-in-Residence for the National Conference of Christians and Jews.

PREFACE

The following essays in collaboration have a somewhat lengthy history. Begun in 1969 by David Tracy, they have been revised, to be taken up finally by Stephen Happel in 1981–82. Yet they would never have been completed except for the constant vigilance of their (more than) editor, Carl Hermann Voss. His ecumenical concern oversaw the project through multiple shifts in geography, scholarly attention, and personal trials. This book owes its existence to his dedication.

Over the years, however, partners in dialogue have engendered new thoughts, turned to different projects, and become interested in specialized issues. The political and religious situations have drawn the participants to more immediate topics. In such an environment, collaboration means many things. Two people have obviously worked together, contributing their judgments about Catholicism, negotiating compromises where disagreement was inevitable, shaping a whole which belongs to both of us together and to neither of us separately.

Beyond this, however, a deeper common effort emerged. Once teacher and student, we are now colleagues in an academic community. Since at this writing one of us is a professor in an urban university, the other a teacher at a seminary and pastor of a rural parish, we have for long spoken to the widely varying publics (academic, confessional, and societal) that join our religious world. As members of diocesan presbyterates (Bridgeport, Connecticut and Indianapolis, Indiana), we are convinced of an ecclesial responsibility to manifest God's Word to modern society.

From within our respective fields of vision, we have hoped to write a book that will appeal to literate inquirers—those who are surveying one of the major understandings of Christianity. The volume, however, is not a scholar's history, a specialist's position on the nature of the Church. It is not a catechism of Catholic doctrine or a systematic treatise on theological ideas.

We have written a rhetorical invitation to the meaning of Catholic life. Taking from other writers information about dates and places, interpretations concerning particular episodes, and judgments on individuals, movements, and their purposes, we have woven together materials which display designs of value to believer and nonbeliever alike. Like all rhetoric, however, our presentation involves partial argumentation and selective examples, though we believe that what is incomplete here can be described more fully, argued perhaps more cogently, and envisioned in more partisan fashion in other works. Here we have a story of what has been "going forward" during the formation of the Catholic tradition.

The view of the Church which follows can be only a single frame of a developing picture, the final composition of which awaits Divine action. If we awaken interest in what this Church may have to say to our world, if we can offer to the many honest searchers for meaning a hope that here there is some significant value, if we show believers that trusting their own story can revitalize their beliefs, then we shall have succeeded. We shall have encouraged others to share with us a Catholic vision which continues to inspire our faith, to nurture our hope, and to enable our love in a world which sorely requires all three.

Stephen Happel   David Tracy
St. Meinrad School of Theology   The Divinity School
St. Meinrad, Indiana   The University of Chicago

Advent, 1982

ACKNOWLEDGMENTS

To accomplish our task, we were grateful for the willing help of Ephrem Carr, Cyprian Davis, Colman Grabert, John Huckle, and James Walter, each of whom contributed clarity of thought and correction of fact. Jackie Culpepper, Ava Gehlhausen, Shirley Kurtzhals, Shirley Risinger, and Andrew Wimmer provided inestimable technical assistance. Irena Makarushka completed the careful index. The errors that remain, the choice of particulars through which we have chosen to see the whole—all these continue to be our own. The volume is dedicated to our nieces and nephews, brothers and sisters with whom we have learned Catholicism and who will in turn continue that Tradition in their actions and speech.

1

WHAT IS CATHOLICISM?

Glory be to God for dappled things—
Gerard Manley Hopkins (1844–89), "Pied Beauty"

Catholicism is a classic. Some would say, of course, that like a dinosaur, it should remain a museum piece to spark the brushfires of the child's imagination about the past. Others speak of it as though it were a laboratory specimen to be preserved so that its analyzed entrails might foretell the exact detail of our religious future. Still others read its story from cover to cover, find a quaint dust jacket, and believe that they can place it back on its shelf, going about their religious business without further attention to its program.

But a true classic will allow none of these dismissals of its power. An authentic artifact provokes those who would ignore it, piques the interest of those who wish to examine it disinterestedly, and surprises those who think they have it easily labeled. Michelangelo's *Pietà* is such a stunning work of art; so are Cervantes's *Don Quixote,* Palestrina's *Motets on the Song of Songs,* Shakespeare's *King Lear,* and the Monet *Water Lilies.* There are authoritative people, such as Joan of Arc or Thomas Jefferson; events such as D-Day in Normandy or Brutus's killing of Caesar; architecture like the Taj Mahal or the cathedral at Chartres; even places of natural beauty like the English Lake Country or the Grand Canyon.

Such persons, places, and things startle us by their continuing need to be experienced, understood, absorbed into our lives. They compel us into arguments with those who disagree with us (for example, about the meaning of Adolf Hitler or Franklin Roosevelt); they sometimes frighten us by their power over us (like the nuclear bomb); or they console us through remembered pleasure and anticipated comfort (like a favorite piece of music). They cannot be heedlessly discarded whatever we think, feel, or do.

Catholicism cannot be ignored. Whether we are one of those who detest it because we think it a monolithic tyranny or whether we

1

welcome it as the most varied interpretation of the Christ-event, we cannot but be impressed by its amazing energy. No one who witnessed any of Pope John Paul II's tours of Poland, the United States, or Middle and South America can deny the extraordinary appeal this man's religious Tradition generates. No one who anxiously watched television after he was made the victim of an assassin's bullets can disregard the emotional value for which he stands. The papal role in the contemporary Catholic Church is a powerful witness to the strength of this religious Tradition.

But the present pope of Polish background is only one surprise among many in recent years in the Catholic Church. What once seemed a stolid, squatting giant has suddenly been transformed into a corps de ballet—a troupe of multicultural dancers who do not always seem to follow the same choreographer. Yet the diversity that is more obvious to us now, due to contemporary communications, can be turned like a telescope onto the history of Catholicism as a whole. Looking back through the centuries, we find armadas and rosaries, councils and inquisitions, medieval crusades and papal pleas against the nuclear arms race, revolutionary clerics and military chaplains blessing battleships. Catholicism is all of these and more.

It is *more* because if all these differing realities were simply relayed to us as so many beads on a string, they would not disclose the religious energies that generated all these events, peoples, and things. For Catholicism is not simply a cultural classic of the first order: it is a *religious* standard. Religious events or people claim to speak not about a part of reality, but about the Whole. They prod us into dialogue with that Whole; they disclose the one Voice without which we cannot hear our own words; they proclaim themselves as the gift of that Speaker within all languages.

Religion discloses this ultimate mystery through the experiences of death, estrangement, the absurdities of existence, the trust or wonder invited by the world, the simple sense of "something more" to reality, and the experience of a love which knows no restrictions or conditions. This experiential focus will determine the particular symbols, stories, or themes in which authors embody their religious meaning. But in each case, on the other side of death and sin, a sense of the uncanny or all-consuming love appears as the gifted dimension of life.

That graciousness may threaten our authenticity or confirm our moral generosity—but it stubbornly refuses our attempts to limit its scope or power. It commands at the same time that it frees. Catholicism is that sort of religious classic. Throughout its history, it could rarely be ignored.

CATHOLICISM AS A CLASSIC

Catholicism is nothing without its history. Its religious understanding of Christianity is wedded to its own experience as the presence of the original event of Jesus. Not only is it based upon the one crucial moment of the life, death, and resurrection of Jesus of Nazareth as portrayed in the Jewish and Christian Scriptures, but it believes the history of its own community to be the preservation and re-presentation of his transforming presence.

Re-presentation will always mean the making present of a reality that occurred uniquely in the past, disclosing in the present the core or essence of a particular event, recognizing God's universal Presence in time and space. The substance of Catholicism is presented again in each age—but always embodied in new events and people. The authentic religious experience does not simply repeat itself, but appears in newly divined circumstances as the same God in different presentations.

The Christian Scriptures look to specific years (about 6 B.C.E.– 33 C.E.)[1] in an out-of-the-way place (Palestine) in the Roman Empire as decisive for all times and places. The Gospels do not pretend to be historical or biographical in the same way we ordinarily take those words. They are interpretations of the significance of Jesus' life and death for the early disciples of Christ—a bold announcement inaugurated by faith in a living Lord risen from the dead. And because these convictions about Jesus are clothed in religious symbols, stories, and concepts which were vibrant for first-century Jewish or Hellenistic audiences, they remain far from us in place and time. But we have the uncanny sense upon hearing these texts that the events are of earth-shattering importance—to be left aside only at the peril of our whole being. God acted here in history; he can be spurned only out of ignorance or malice.

CATHOLIC HISTORY: TRADITION

Catholicism's perennial vigor is due to its belief in that particular history and its own ability to embody that original event. It is in and through the history of its successive transformations that Catholics find the meaning of their religion. By interpretations of the past and ongoing anticipations of the future, Catholics commit themselves to the re-presentation of their Lord. This living frame of reference the Catholic calls *Tradition*. Removed from the rituals, texts, persons, and institutions which continue to present that Tradition, Catholics feel lost, dislocated, exiled. Catholics are at home in history.

Recent Catholic theology, philosophical as well as biblical, has focused on the ideas about history which join the parts of this book. They are drawn from the heart of Jesus' preaching: the coming of the Kingdom of God into world history. As an academic subject, it has been called *eschatology* (from the Greek *eschata* meaning "last things"), since it dealt with the final events of the cosmic process. More recently, however, eschatology has included the broader meaning of Jesus for the history of our world in all its dimensions.

This religious sense of history has not always been the center of Catholic theology; and the path to change has not always been easy. It will be helpful for us to recall here some of the factors which have shaped this shift in Catholic thinking—particularly since they affect this book.

Shaping Our Destiny

There is first a widely recognized move from classicist to historical consciousness.[2] Since the nineteenth century, we experience ourselves as the shapers of our own lives. Not only do we pass through history, but we are made by that history. The past weighs us down or liberates us; the future pushes us forward or into shock; and the present is a moment of decision, of the possible rejection or acceptance of past and future.

Not only need we not always be the way we were, but it might be

4

critical enough to make a revolution in the present so that we can live a completely different future. The political revolutions of 1776 in the colonies of England in North America and of 1789 in France liberated the personal power of individuals and classes to think that the world could be other than it was. And even if in our revised history the darker side of each revolution has tempered the original enthusiasm, these events still appeal to us, telling us that there can be something *new* if we help it to happen.

Science and Religion

But this shift from a consciousness which thought of the world, peoples, and the social order as necessary and unchanging occurred first among scientists. It was Aristotle, then Newton, who studied the world for its abstract, eternal laws, convinced that they were tapping the unmoving structures of reality. Contemporary scientists, however, have more modest goals. They inquire into what is probable, what can be empirically verified. Instead of searching for *the* essential, changeless universe, we are content to live with the best scientific opinion.

Christian theology is disciplined reflection upon religion in a specific culture. As a result, it is affected by the notions about thinking held by scientists and philosophers of culture. Through the framework of a changeless science, our ancestors could experience the harmony and power of the world as a religious event. But one of the prime goals of modern science was the harnessing of nature for practical purposes. Early scientific experiments such as those concerning gases were tried so that eventually their power might be made to work for us. Technology has always been an intertwined means and end in modern science.

As a result, nature is no longer so alien to us. It may still provoke awe, as for example when Mt. St. Helens erupts; but it does not invite us to the same religious experience of eternity. We are stirred by the thrill of scientific discovery, by the impact of political events, by the marvel of international communication, and by the tragedies and successes of forming human community. We can only recover the religious meaning of nature through the discovery of the transcendent value of the transitory, the historical.

5

Historical Overload

New cultures are born in our midst and the oldest ones die or are exterminated by industrial "progress." What happens in Nigeria can be seen simultaneously in New York. At the same time that we are exploring other planets and planning journeys to the moon, we wonder somewhat breathlessly whether we can halt the destruction on our own planet. Constantly bombarded by these phenomena, we have begun to feel not only how fleeting our experience is—but also how much the sheer weight of data in our computer banks oppresses us. Our identity escapes us in all the diverse demands of modern culture. If our ancestors could say, "The more things change, the more they stay the same," we can no longer fully believe that.

THE HISTORICAL NATURE OF FAITH

The historical dimension of modern experience has forced the leading minds in Christian communities to employ scientific methods for the study of their own past. Through these critical investigations, we have come to understand and interpret the Christian experience itself. Results have confirmed the deeply temporal nature of our New Testament faith. The Jewish and Christian God is not primarily a deity of nature or of nature's unchangeable laws. Rather God is One who acts in time, who leads people through history. God is that One who encounters men and women exhausted and exhilarated by events and draws them toward love through just such times and seasons. It is this living God of promise and of hope to whom Jews and Christians pray and for whom Jews and Christians search again in this century. If we are to discover our God at all, we must find the Divine Presence in the public stories of peoples, nations, and churches.

Our immediate past has made Christians' involvement in history even more compelling. No sooner did the soothing, ultimately deadly optimism of nineteenth-century Europe collapse in the dreadful trenches of World Wars than Christian theologians began to wonder how theology could live so comfortably with the myths of progress (and so later with the unspeakable horrors of Nazism). The knowledge of change, of the constantly shifting human condition, drew

Christians inward. Turning from the public world of nature, education, and politics, fearful of confronting what they could not control, they valued the private loyalties, the familial virtues, and the intimate loves. This can and did lead to insularity, isolationism, narcissism, and a mere nostalgia for the past. But it was easier to live inside the Church than to bear the crushing controversies of war, nuclear arms, the depletion of resources, and the economic exploitation of Third and Fourth World countries. Christianity was reduced to a "private" classic, a cultural Church that had forgotten its own past. But its religious power has stubbornly refused suicide.

Catholicism sometimes retreated into the privatized world of personal piety; but its commitment to its own public institutional face has more often prohibited neglect of the world. Some may not have agreed with Pius IX's rejection of contemporary values (*Syllabus of Errors*, 1864), Leo XIII's support for the just wage (*Rerum Novarum*, 1891), Paul VI's understanding of marriage and contraception (*Humanae Vitae*, 1968), or his judgments on private property (*Populorum Progressio*, 1967); but over the last one hundred years, the Catholic community has juxtaposed itself to culture with intransigent opposition, hearty acceptance, or critical persuasiveness.

American Catholics have been forced by the cultural acceptance of abortion, the public defense of the wars in southeast Asia, or the support of authoritarian regimes in South and Middle America to reexamine their own complacent histories. Catholics know that their fears and hopes are shared by commentators in the United States as well. Assassinations, attempted and achieved; race riots; uncontrolled inflation; severe unemployment among minority groups; foreign policies that ignore human rights—each in its own way has pushed Catholics into a new search for the God of their history. It is no pastime of the ivory tower.

UPDATING THE CHURCH

The Second Vatican Council (1962–65), called by Pope John XXIII, gathering all the Catholic bishops of the world to "bring [the church] up to date" (*aggiornamento*), encouraged Catholics to rethink and relive the relationship between themselves and their cultures. *The Pastoral Constitution on the Church in the Modern World* (1965) announced that the "joys and the hopes, the griefs and the anxieties of the men of this age, especially those who are poor or in any way afflicted, these too are the joys and hopes, the griefs and anxieties of the followers of Christ. Indeed, nothing genuinely human fails to raise an echo in their hearts."[3]

This deepened sense of our own world, the sharpened tools of historical criticism, the alienation from nature as a vehicle for religion, and the overarching shift in the classicist notion of an unchanging science have challenged Catholics to reenvision their own community. For the Roman Catholic Church is not meant to be merely one more institution standing with equal dispassion alongside the other institutions of our society.

Whatever concrete structures the Church has, or has had, have been intended to serve the proclamation of the New Testament history. The structure has meant to be a reflection of a living, continuous community of ritual, morality, and doctrine. We cannot naively identify this concrete Church through the ages with the full realization of the New Testament Kingdom of God. Rather, the Church knows itself to be the servant of that approaching Kingdom, obedient to its Word and committed to the faithful sowing of that Word in the soil of history. "The Church seeks but a solitary goal: to carry forward the work of Christ Himself under the lead of the befriending Spirit."[4]

Once we realize this, the Catholic Tradition becomes less important institutionally, but more significant religiously. The Church can be experienced as the *community* of those awaiting God in history. Indeed, it is precisely this experience of God's Future communicated to those who wrote the New Testament and to the figures who followed in the history of Catholicism which forms the *community* of eschatological hope.

The Church for Catholics is primarily an event, not a thing. It is the place where all peoples communally may celebrate the Good News of God's actions for all. It is the space where we allow ourselves to be judged by the demands of a genuine religious life. It is—at its best—always reforming itself, "always living and always young," as Pope John XXIII stated in his convocation of the Second Vatican Council. The Church "feels the rhythm of the times and . . . in every

8

century beautifies herself with new splendor, radiates new light, achieves new conquests, while remaining identical in herself, faithful to the divine image impressed on her countenance by her Spouse, Who loves her and protects her, Christ Jesus."[5]

OUR PROJECT

It is this *cumulative* identity of the ecclesial community that this book hopes to outline. Neither of us as the authors of this book pretends to be a historian; both of us believe that it is possible to interpret the life of the Church in such a way that the ongoing story of the community can enlighten the religious meaning of our wider culture.

As a cumulative experience, Catholicism has often been accused of being totalitarian or uncritical of its own history. In the chapters that follow, we hope to provide a largely *typological* interpretation of Catholicism. It is like tracing the major events of particular ages on sheets of transparent plastic and placing them one on top of the other so that at the end we can look through the centuries and see the overlapping identity. For Catholicism's history, like that of an individual, can be secured only at the end; and the end is God's work, not ours.

Throughout our study, we will indicate some of the demands made upon the New Testament experience by events and issues within and without the Church. In doing so, we do not think that the Christian experience was collapsed into contemporary cultural demands. We simply believe that religious values and norms must be embodied to be seen and heard. As a result, it is only as the centuries move on that some subjects even appear on the scene. For example, the whole notion of *eschatology* (Jesus' meaning for human history) is largely a nineteenth- and twentieth-century interpretive tool. That does not mean that people did not think of historical events or of the end times until then, only that it became an explicit subject for investigation at about that time.[6]

Catholic identity is a constantly emergent sense of new experience, and how that newness may be confronted, absorbed, and Christianized. Catholics believe in the development of ever new events happening to all those who share God's promise of redemption. This

9

means that not only in the past, but in the present and the future, the message of Jesus Christ will initiate ever remarkable and radically wondrous possibilities.

The story of these experiences for Catholics—past and present—will be our concern in the remainder of this book. Religious people ask: "What is the meaning of the Whole?" "Is it possible to be responsible for our lives in the face of death?" The community's struggles with and answers to those religious questions unroll as the story of Catholicism. The authentic responses to the questions embodied in the people, places, and things which appear in its history manifest themselves as the servant of the Kingdom, as the shining sacrament of his Presence.

NOTES

1. In deference to our Jewish, Islamic, and Buddhist coreligionists, we will not employ A.D. (in the year of the Lord) and B.C. (before Christ), but B.C.E. (before the Common Era) and C.E. (Common Era).

2. Bernard Lonergan, *Method in Theology* (London: Darton, Longman & Todd, 1972), 2, 29, 301–2, 305–19.

3. "Pastoral Constitution on the Church in the Modern World," *Vatican Council II: The Conciliar and Post-Conciliar Documents*, ed. Austin Flannery (Northport, N.Y.: Costello, 1975), 903–5.

4. Ibid.

5. "Humanae Salutis," December 25, 1961, in *The Documents of Vatican II*, ed. Walter Abbott (New York: Guild Press, 1966), 706.

6. See fig. 1, p. 183 for an image of the fields of theology as they emerged throughout Catholic history.

2

THE EMERGENCE OF
CATHOLIC CHRISTIANITY (I)
Images, Symbols, and Stories:
New Testament Catholicism

> Son of God, have pity on us
> And do with us according to thy kindness,
> And bring us out from the bonds of darkness:
> And open to us the door by which we shall
>   come out to thee.
> Let us also be redeemed with thee:
> For thou are our Redeemer.
> And I heard their voice;
> And my name I sealed upon their heads:
> For they are free men and they are mine.
> Hallelujah.
>
> Anon., *Odes of Solomon* (about 150 C.E.)

Christian identity began in Galilean images and stories opposed by Jews and Greeks alike. Yet by the early fourth century, it had the tolerance, then approval, of the Roman Empire. The known world heard the Gospel proclaimed. What had provoked this amazing growth? What are the crucial elements in the original experience that encouraged the event of Jesus of Nazareth to take the shape of a transracial, transnational community? The transformation of a Jewish movement into the categories of the Greco-Roman world is in many ways a most distinctly Catholic development. For "Catholic" means, first of all, "universal."

During the first three centuries, emerging Catholicism was a complicated affair. What is clear, however, is that imperial citizens, in accepting those whom they formerly persecuted, introduced their own cultural experience into Christianity. How Christians rebuilt that culture into Catholic truth is the subject of this and the two following chapters.

11

THE PATTERNS OF NEW TESTAMENT EXPRESSION

Let us probe more deeply in the Christian Scriptures themselves to communicate a basic, recurring pattern within the plural expressions that interpret the classic event of Jesus. Since we are concentrating on a Church which defines itself in terms of history, we should meditate a few moments on time itself.

Apprehending Time

Each one of us would like to capture a moment or two in our lives. We never want to repeat the ordinary, boring minutes but rather the cheerful times. All too often, we remember being jailed behind the bars of unpleasant, even tragic, hours. Yet what we discover is that in no way can we isolate atomic moments, embalming them so that they can be viewed in the round, pinned to a piece of cardboard like a butterfly. Time continues to live in us. There are no disconnected moments, only a series of presents which contain within them the shadings of memory, custom, and education, and the hoped-for projections of fears, desires, needs, and plans. The present is thick, pregnant with the children of our past and heavy with the adolescents and adults of our future.

Sometimes we find that the past dominates the present moment, so powerful is our memory. Whole societies can be entranced with their own pasts, as in the United States when the Revolution of 1776 or the Civil War are recalled. The past can also cripple our actions in the present: for example, when we remember the guilty time of our betrayal of a friend. Often the loss of someone we love virtually stops all motion, making our lives vibrate to the tunes of pain and grief.

The future can also drag us unwillingly from the present. Occasionally our daydreams, our projects, our images for economic success or societal utopia seize us with such passion that the immediate context dissolves. Our daydreams become nightmares, visions of nuclear desolation and corpselike certainty. The present recedes into dreadful fascination with a future over which we have little control.

Gabriel Garcia Marquez's *One Hundred Years of Solitude* epitomizes our contemporary attitude toward time. In Macondo, a tropical Brazilian *Erewhon,* time crystallizes into a multifaceted jewel, a phantasmagoric dream, in which we see the ancient colonial decades and Indian magic through an enigmatic prism of present and future. We are never quite certain in what part of the time machine we have arrived. The bizarre effect of this novel reveals our present in which stone-age nomadic cultures abut urban villages like Brazilia. It is as though the whole history of our world were suddenly simultaneous—the past and future concentrated into a distilled present whose liquor we can drink with our morning news.

Biblical Time

But so it has always been with the classic documents of our Tradition. Time comes alive in their present as a memory which shadows us now and as a future which sometimes hectors us when we least expect it. The same was true with the community of Christians when they lived, wrote, and dwelt within the Scriptures. The images which dominate the New Testament—the Kingdom of God, the heavenly Jerusalem, the mustard seed, the pearl of great price, and preeminently the stories of the cross and resurrection—have shaped the Church's memories and anticipations.

Sometimes the presence of the Risen Lord has so overwhelmed believers that they can but sing, pray, and prophesy. Speaking their own words, but caught up in the presence of the Divine, they cry out with God's voice. For the prophets it was a matter of being addressed by God in the very moment of their own speaking.

Remembering their origins, communities celebrated the Lord in ritual, preaching, and sacrament. From this strong sense of God's presence came stories about the past of their God. The narrative traditions were embedded in a dialogue with the Risen Christ. Believing themselves Jews for whom the Messiah and his age had come, they related their founding event to those who would listen. Building upon the covenant given to Abraham, Isaac, and Jacob, they knew their Lord to be the *already* of a Kingdom which had *not yet* come, the first fruits of those who would enter the Holiness of God. It was not an uprooting of the promises made to Israel, but a new grafting to the Ancient Vine of David.

But sometimes the community became so frustrated that their only religious option longed for the future when God would right all the social and personal wrongs of the present. During this messianic age, the humble Prophet crucified like a thief would reveal himself as the Lord of glory.

Catholic history is founded in this New Testament experience of the *prophetic,* the *traditional,* and the *apocalyptic* (named for the Greek word for revelation). One or another of these moments has always shaped Catholic life, like an idea in the mind of a sculptor. Occasionally the conversation among these temporal moments has been a debate or even a battle. But what has marked Catholicism most is its yearning to encompass all partners in a creative dialogue. When the attempts have failed, Catholicism has cheated itself of its own universality.

The Prophetic Word

In our Jewish heritage, prophets are those for whom God is so real and powerful a presence that they cannot *but* use their tongues as though they were burned by a fiery coal. Nothing—honor, fame, career, money, even life itself—means more than being aflame with God's power of proclamation. All the usual distractions of life are only so many temptations away from the consuming presence of Yahweh. Whether it is manifesting God's presence through some symbolic action (as Isaiah did by walking through Jerusalem naked! Isa. 20:2ff) or preaching in fierce rhetoric the judgment of God's coming victory over the evils of sin, the prophet can do no other.

Jewish and Christian prophets proclaim the thrust of God's Kingdom into our world. In a series of startling figures such as Isaiah, Jeremiah, Amos, Hosea, Ezekiel, John the Baptist, and culminating in Jesus of Nazareth, the Christian Tradition is claimed by the Word of God. Each individual, in his own particular voice, manifested the presence of God to and in the people. By threatening military defeat (Jer. 1:14), by an overwhelming welcoming love for the sinful (Hos. 1:2), or by demanding repentance because the axe was laid to the root of social evil (Matt. 3:9–10), every prophet announced that life without God was vanity and illusion. The past and the future seemed relatively unimportant as long as people would hear God's voice in the *now.*

But the qualifier "relatively" is vital since no authentic Christian or Hebrew prophet ignored the past or neglected the future of God's salvation for the people. The prophets' present understanding and awareness of God allow them to absorb the traditions of their people and to await the future as the action of God alone. In fact, the very authenticity of prophets is bound up in their ability to reinterpret the

14

nation's past in continuity with God's present word and to anticipate with singular vision what God has prepared for the world.

It is not so much that prophets "foretell" the future as that they are so committed to the truth of God's present that their words as God's words sow the seeds of the authentic future. Ralph Waldo Emerson once remarked: "An institution is the lengthened shadow of one man." Such individuals found communities by their forthright speech and we call them prophets. These are the creative, originating heroes and heroines of faith.

For Christians, such an individual was Jesus of Nazareth. The *presence* of God manifested in his actions and words was so powerfully transforming that all later Christian prophets speak in *his* name. He alone makes their prophetic comments a possibility. Our expectations of life—security, comfort, happiness—are shattered when we are faced with this eschatological Prophet who faithfully lived the final power of God even in death itself. God's voice disclosed in Jesus constantly drives Christians into a world that needs to be reformed according to Divine love. The witness that believers give is modeled upon, rooted in, and empowered by this Divine Man, this human Face of God.

The Traditional Story

But a heightened sense of the presence of the Lord, an intense awareness of a transforming energy, can also be present in the memories of the community. For the events of Jesus' life, death, and resurrection need to be told and retold as witness to his prophetic ministry. The stories of his existence which we call the Gospels (*Euangelion*—the Good News) were written to preserve this dangerous memory.

The memory about Jesus is dangerous because it constantly calls into question the status quo. These Gospels, reflecting the concerns of various Christian communities, offer comment upon, and application to, the foundation times of the Churches. They proclaimed the continuity of Jesus' presence in the history of the believing communities. They made it clear that it was God who was acting in Jesus; it was God who was calling believers to witness by service to the world and loving generosity to one another.

The language of Jesus' story, therefore, became the paradigm for the common life. His prayerfulness (the "Our Father") was the prayer of the Church; his Tradition of learning (the Hebrew Scriptures—the "Old" Testament) became the interpretive categories of the "New" Covenant made by God. All Christians could have Christ's meaning available to them in prayer, worship, sacrament, the gifts of leadership and office, creedal doctrines, and the narratives of the Good News.

Some of the genius of Catholicism lies in its ability to live what is possible for men and women as they are. Although not everyone is given the strength to be prophetic, all are called to be religious. Catholics can live holy lives by belonging to that community, the Church, which keeps the dangerous memory of its religious origins not just intact, but always renewed through Word and sacrament. The interplay of prophets, office-holders, ordinary pray-ers, visionaries, preachers, and thinkers, in which each accomplishes his or her unique witness to Christ *is* the rich strength of the Catholic Church.

In the New Testament itself, this development can be seen in "emergent Catholicism"—the growth of offices such as deacon, presbyter, and bishop who govern the community, protecting it from errors of content in the memory of Jesus (1 Tim. 3:1–13, Titus 1:5–7). The experience of doctrinal confession discloses a somewhat different world from that of the prophetic witness. There is an emphasis upon the information of our confession; the shock of Jesus' proverbs, parables, and sayings about the End Times has shifted toward specific applications, moral prescriptions, and clear beliefs. It is an honoring of the everyday character of the religious enterprise, the manifestation and proclamation of God's presence in Jesus' daily gift of table fellowship to outcasts and ordinary sinners.

This traditional Catholic manner of remembering the vitality of Jesus is in fact a social and intellectual fence around the original witness. It is a hedge against forgetting. But that does not mean that it is somehow a secondary element in the New Testament experience.

The institutional forms of office, doctrine, gospel, or ritual are the authentic presence of the risen Lord. If they seem less intense, that is due more to our human tendency to screen out their conversation with prophetic charism, the tension of symbols, and the ecstatic prayer of longing for God. In dialogue with these elements in the

New Testament, Catholics believe that each authentically re-presents the Christ event.

The Apocalyptic Vision

In addition, however, to the prophetic and traditional elements in the Christian experience, there is a third factor which looks more directly toward the future. It is the apocalyptic, named for the Greek word meaning revelation (*apocalypsis*). It is a name usually given to the final text in the New Testament, the Book of Revelation.

Apocalyptic literature is provoked in times of utter crisis (for example, during persecution or social destruction). When the world seems ready to implode, apocalypse announces the coming Reign of God, the victory of Divine Presence over evil. It does so through dreams, visions, and symbolic descriptions of warfare between good and the powers of evil.

The apocalyptic thread in the New Testament is a major theme in Jesus' own proclamation of the coming reign of God. The Son of Man will judge the living and the dead at the End Times. The seer of the Book of Revelation expects a new heaven and a new earth after the conflicts and persecutions which will anticipate the end. The apocalyptic visionary always throws a challenge at the community, a rebuttal to any complacency which has crept into its experience. The *real* hope for the Churches is not their mediations of Jesus through texts, offices, or rites; rather the true future is God's in Christ. The vision constantly corrects all other expressions of Christian meaning, for everything is risked on the future.

We tend to think of individuals who constantly expect the reversal of common hopes and dreams as too pessimistic, too other-worldly. But events themselves can provoke this shift in religious awareness. There are times in history—the period 200 B.C.E. to 100 C.E., during which the stories of the New Testament took place, is one of these—when prophets are rare, traditions in question, and the present is riddled with calamities. Then only God's future seems to have any significance. One's hope—that God will remain faithful to the world—requires trust in a future that God alone controls and transforms all history.

Early Christians, during the decades of ecclesial formation and particularly with the destruction of Jerusalem (70 C.E.), sensed such

17

an apocalyptic moment. Only the Father of the Lord Jesus could save them from the Roman armies. It is not surprising that apocalyptic Christianity has recently revived in a world in which ordinary believers feel that their very daily lives have been snatched from their control. Wars and the rumors of war thrust Christians into a future known only to God.

No matter what we may think of the contemporary suffering of humanity and certain assessments that all mediations, religious and otherwise, have fallen short or even failed, we know that the apocalyptic response is an authentically religious one. We may find visionaries strange and seers all too fallible—but we know that they form one of the partners in the conversation of Catholicism. Without the criticism offered by those who can only see the *not yet* of God's presence, Christianity too easily forgets the dangerous character of its own past and lists becalmed in the ship of a complacent present.

Jesus of Nazareth provoked all three responses: the prophetic, the traditional, and the apocalyptic. In hymns, stories, sayings, letters, and theological meditations, the presence of this Jesus comes forward to encounter the believer. Now one temporal dimension, now another, will dominate. But each helped form the community of believers who followed the Nazarene. The Presence of God to and in the man Jesus—a Presence which for the Catholic *is* his Identity— proclaims him as Lord of all time: past, present, and future. His history is the model of individual and social stories; the history of his Presence founds the community of that Presence.

Saintly Heroes

We shall look at three early figures in Catholicism who tell us about its developments in the New Testament: Peter, Paul, and Stephen the Martyr. The character of later Christianity is clearly informed by these remarkable individuals.

Peter, Leader of the Twelve

We actually know very little about the life of Peter. Aside from his legendary background as a fisherman (Mark 1:16–18), we know only that invariably he is located first in the lists of the disciples (Matt. 10:2), and that he regularly took the lead, becoming the mouthpiece for the Twelve, as when he says that they could not leave

Jesus (John 6:66–69). At Caesarea Philippi, his confession of Jesus' Messiahship earned him the name Peter and a role of authority in the coming Kingdom (the keys to the palace—Matt. 16:13–20).

Peter was, however, a thoroughly "ordinary" individual, whose enthusiasm (John 18:10) and subsequent denial of Christ during his passion and death (Matt. 26:33f) signify his utterly human abilities. According to the Gospel of Luke (Luke 24:34), he was granted a special appearance of the risen Christ; and this conscious awareness made him the first preacher on Pentecost (Acts 2:14–41), a miracle worker in the name of Jesus (Acts 3:1–10), and a speaker before the Sanhedrin (Acts 4:1–21).

Early traditions placed Peter's death in Rome during the persecution after Nero's burning of the city (65 C.E.). It is as saint and martyr, and as first missionary apostle of Rome, that Catholic Christians honor Peter as the first pope. This great man, so fallible, so faithful to the Lord, so relatively obscure, still seems to capture the imagination of Christians. For Peter is honored as that rarest of religious phenomena: a holy leader whose humane moderation, whose "common touch," created a powerful Tradition. It is to just such a figure that Pope John XXIII (1958–63) appealed when he established a Secretariat for Promoting Christian Unity (1960) and had the Catholic Church represented at the World Council of Churches (1961). When Pope John Paul II tapped his foot during a rally with youth in Yankee Stadium in New York City (1980), Peter's missionary and prophetic humanity was again announced.

Paul, Apostle to the Gentiles

Peter's great counterpart and occasional antagonist (Gal. 2:6–9) is Paul, or Saul of the tribe of Benjamin. Paul remains to historical eyes the most forceful personality in early ecclesial life. If Peter's great claim is to be the founder of an ecclesiastical Tradition, Paul's untiring gift of his person in missionary journeys, in writing letters (or epistles), and in producing a theology that justified his turning to Gentiles to fill the ranks of Christians marks him as the co-Apostle of the founded Church.

But Paul was not always an Apostle, that is, one sent to preach the Good News and to found Christian communities. He had been a persecutor of the Christian Jews; and only after an intense experi-

19

ence of conversion (Acts 9:1–19, 22:5–16, 26:12–18), in which he saw the Risen Lord in his persecuted followers, did he choose to devote his life to Christianity. He was baptized and retired to Arabia for solitude and prayer. Three years later he returned to Damascus and Jerusalem.

The Christian community at Antioch sent him on the first of his missionary journeys. Throughout his life, he traveled ceaselessly and tirelessly preached the Gospel throughout the Mediterranean world. He seems to have died in Rome during the persecution of Nero (about 65 C.E.) in which Peter himself was killed.

In the letters to various Churches Paul founded or visited, we have the first great Christian theology. For he labored at that crucial problem of the early communities, the relationship between the Christ and Jewish religious life under the Law. In his confrontation with Peter (described schematically as the First Council of Jerusalem in Acts of the Apostles 15), Paul won Gentile converts the right to neglect certain prescriptions of Jewish ceremonial and religious law. For example, circumcision was no longer required of the baptized Christian male.

Yet Paul says later (Rom. 9:1–5) that he would even be willing to be separated from Christ if his own brothers, the Israelites, could be reconciled. "Theirs was the adoption, the glory, the covenants, the lawgiving, the worship, and the promises; theirs were the patriarchs, and from them came the Messiah" (Rom. 9:4–5, NAB).

For Paul, Christian Gospel had liberated us from the Law by a sheer gift of God's grace. In Christ, the world's purpose finds its goal (Phil. 2:6; Col. 1:15–17). He is the Lord of a new humanity which replaces the old Adam of our failures. One need no longer be under the power of sin, since a new energy, an enabling gift, has entered our world in Christ's death and resurrection. Through baptism we receive and confirm this gift (Rom. 6:3–6) and accept God's own Spirit whose charity binds the common herd into a community of Churches. The signal action of this community is the great Thanksgiving, the Eucharist (1 Cor. 10:16–21; 11:20–34), in which the one sacrifice of Jesus is remembered and re-presented. But all this is to see but darkly; one day we shall see our God face to face (1 Corinthians 13).

Paul's ability to view the past event of Jesus' death as present and to proclaim it, his conviction that this risen Presence would soon return, and his knowledge of the human heart in all its stark confusion has allowed him to confront each age of Christians. The literary and religious power of his letters has founded prophets, theologies, and Churches. Without his prophetic vision, Christians could have confined themselves to the original Semitic experience and ignored the ethical responsibility to the *not yet* character of the future coming of the Lord.

Stephen, the Martyr

At Paul's origins stands Stephen's murder. For while still a persecutor of Christians, he is said to have tended the garments of those who stoned Stephen. Stephen was probably a Hellenistic Jew who was chosen as one of Seven to serve tables in the Jerusalem community (Acts 6:5). He cared for the needy, preached the Gospel, and performed miracles, earning the hostility of the local non-Hellenistic population. In the beautiful homiletic set piece recorded in Acts 7:2–53, Stephen recalls all of Israel's history as leading to *the* Prophet announced by Moses, one Jesus who was killed on a cross. For his preaching efforts, he was made the first Christian martyr.

Before he died, however, he saw the glory of God returning (Acts 7:54–56) and Jesus at God's right hand. As he died, he forgave his enemies as did his Lord before him. It was this intensity of vision that forced him from the present into God's future for him.

Peter, Paul, and Stephen, woven together by God in coincidence, conflict, tragedy, and glory through their allegiance to Jesus, demonstrate the contrasting diversities of the founding preachers of Catholicism. For while Paul discloses the burning genius of the fiery preacher and Stephen the socially committed, culturally complicated visionary, Peter displays our steady common humanity. Tradition, prophecy, and apocalypse disclose the intertwining truths of Catholic history. From Jesus, the source, spring Catholic claims to the universe of time and space; in Peter, Paul, and Stephen and a constant current of others flows the abiding history of Catholicism, diversity in unity.

FURTHER RELATED MATERIAL

For a helpful introduction, employing some of the literary-critical methods of interpretation present in this book, see Norman Perrin, *The New Testament: An Introduction* (New York: Harcourt Brace Jovanovich, 1974) and for historical-critical background, see Robert M. Grant, *A Historical Introduction to the New Testament* (London: William Collins Sons, 1963). For various understandings of Jesus in the New Testament, see Gunther Bornkamm, *Jesus of Nazareth* (New York: Harper & Brothers, 1960); Reginald Fuller, *The Foundations of New Testament Christology* (New York: Charles Scribner's Sons, 1965); Edward Schillebeeckx, *Jesus: An Experiment in Christology*, trans. Hubert Hoskins (London: William Collins & Co., 1979) and *Christ: The Experience of Jesus as Lord*, trans. John Bowden (New York: Seabury Press, 1980); and Bruce Vawter, *This Man Jesus: An Essay Toward a New Testament Christology* (Garden City, N.Y.: Doubleday & Co., 1973). Sections of Hans Küng's *On Becoming a Christian*, trans. Edward Quinn (New York: Doubleday & Co., 1976), 145–165 are also useful.

THE EMERGENCE OF
CATHOLIC CHRISTIANITY (II)
The Search for Unity

My Redeemer, redeem me for I am yours;
  from you I came forth.
You are my mind; bring me forth!
You are my treasure-house; open for me!
You are my fullness; take me to you!
You are my repose; give me the perfection
  that cannot be grasped.
        Anon., "Gnostic Prayer of the Apostle Paul" (about 200 C.E.)

It required a lengthy time, at least two hundred years, before Christians began to define themselves according to the writings they had received from their founders. Only between the late second and fourth centuries did a canon, or rule of approved books, come into general use. Early Christian controversies over what exactly constituted an authentic interpretation of the Christ-event were manifold. To understand the development of Catholicism, it is central to our story to have some knowledge of these early movements and the attempts by theologians, churchmen and women, prophets, and martyrs to state *who* the Church was. The directing impulse was not so much to exclude people or interpretations, but rather to care religiously for the truth of the originating event.

We have looked at the primarily Hellenistic forms of Christian experience which emerged in the New Testament literature. But there were at least two other major interpretations which vied with the present canon of Scriptures: specific Semitic forms, generally called Jewish-Christianity, and a largely Greco-Roman religious expression, Gnosticism.

Broadly speaking, we might say that Hebraic or Semitic Christianity did not wish to stress the distance of Christians from Jews which resulted from the Roman destruction of Jerusalem (66–70

23

C.E.) and the expulsion of the adherents of Jesus from the synagogues (70–100 C.E.). Gnostic thought pushed the message of Christ in the direction of cultural identity with the seemingly larger Hellenistic world outside Palestine. Between these two "movements," Christians defined a Tradition offering both criticism of culture and refinement of religious identity. It is this integrated Tradition that is the ongoing history of Catholicism.

JEWISH-CHRISTIANITY

For many years orthodox Jews and believers in Jesus as Lord shared the same general Semitic institutions and literature. Jewish society at the time of Christ was flexibly complex, consisting not only of Pharisees (an austere party which believed in resurrection of the dead and retribution in the next world), Sadducees (strict interpreters of the Mosaic Law), and Essenes (an ascetic, highly organized community in the desert), but also Zealots (anti-Roman agitators), collaborators like the tax collectors, and various Jews of the Diaspora in cosmopolitan cities like Alexandria.

From all these strands, Jean Daniélou and other scholars have isolated Semitic interpretations of Jesus. Jewish-Christianity began as a reforming interpretation of Judaism, but eventually broke its boundaries. Using experiences from the Hebrew Scriptures and apocalyptic literature, it developed a set of organizing images, a narrative to deal with the origins of evil in the universe and the unique event of Jesus. Jesus, the glorious angel of Yahweh, head of the archangels, the very Name of God and preexistent Covenant, redeemed us from the demons of the world by descending into Sheol to preach deliverance to the dead, then ascended into the heavens of God. His cross extended his arms in cosmic hope to all directions of the compass. Raised into the air, Jesus released his Spirit upon all who gazed upon him, recognizing him as Lord.

Using these physical, cosmic pictures, Jewish-Christians stressed adherence to the original Mosaic revelation in the Law, distrusted Paul's grafting of the Gentiles onto Jewish stock and preferred to think of Christ as the Prophet inspired by the Spirit of God. Essentially a conservative Christianity, anxious not to lose its Semitic roots, it branched out toward the East, establishing flourishing centers especially around Edessa and Antioch.

Although there flowered in the third and fourth centuries authentic Semitic theologies in Aphraat (about 260–345) and Ephrem the Syrian (306–73), later stress on the preservation of the Hebraic stories drew these strains into controversy with more Hellenistic Christian language. These believers were ethically austere, often apocalyptic in preaching and uncompromising in their devotion to the Galilean Jesus who had saved them. One of the most ancient forms of our Eucharistic prayer, The Liturgy of Addai and Mari, derives from this Tradition. The earliest important version of the Gospels, the *Diatessaron* (150–60 C.E.), compiled by Tatian (about 160), was a life of Jesus sewn together from all four Gospels. These Christians and their less orthodox relatives continued to inspire converts well into the fourth century.

GNOSIS: PASSIONATE WISDOM

Other groups also assimilated Jesus into their religious and cultural traditions. A deeply Hellenistic movement is called Gnosticism, after the Greek word (*gnosis*) for knowledge. Its origins are controverted and obscure, some authorities maintaining that it appeared prior to Christianity, others contending that it was its product or that of apocalyptic Judaism, still others assuring us that it can be found in early dualisms of the gods of light and darkness. With the discovery of a library of Gnostic texts in Egypt (Nag-Hammadi), we have better information.

A movement of religious combinations, Gnosticism contained elements of Hellenistic Judaism, Babylonian astrology, magic and fatalism, the emerging mystery cults to the gods and goddesses of vegetation, as well as the story and message of Jesus. Gnostics generally thought of Jesus as one who brought them a saving knowledge of God, the true meaning of the world. He came from the purely spiritual fullness of God's power through layers of cosmic confusion to free us from our imprisoned flesh.

The *Hymn of the Pearl,* heavily influenced by Gnosticism, tells the story of a king's son who was sent to Egypt to find the pearl of great price. He arrived only to find the Great Serpent coiled about it in the sea. Having stopped at a local inn, he changed clothes, so that he would not appear strangely dressed. When offered wine he became intoxicated and fell asleep. Awakened by a letter from his royal parents, he returned to his duty. He conquered the serpent, obtained the pearl, and regained his homeland, discarding the garments he received for clothing of transcendent beauty.

This basic story of mission, confusion, recovery, and homecoming became an elaborate system of thought under certain thinkers, such as Valentinus (about 136–165 C.E.). The king's son was sent on an errand of mercy and salvation, only to fall into human existence, a drowsy, drunken state. Lost in forgetfulness he was reminded of his call only by knowledge from another world. As a saved savior he must shed the psychic and physical envelopes which have weighed him down in his journey toward authentic existence.

The descriptive poetry and passionate prayers still have power to alert the inner eyes of consciousness. With the addition of some ritual elements and flexible ethical behavior, Gnosticism maintained a deep hold on Christians. It remains a contemporary possibility where the adage, "Knowledge gives virtue," or even better, "Self-knowledge grants salvation," is still believed.

These conflicting interpretations, together with those we now think of as orthodox, created resounding questions for the growing Christian communities. If this world is an evil one, how is it possible that a good God made it? What is the Christian's relationship to the culture of this age, until Christ returns? If sin is merely ignorance, a mistake or fate, then how do we live as saved? How is Christ uniquely different, if the world keeps going on as before? If God is completely nameless, then how do we know what the relationship of Jesus is to God?

The various answers to these questions created two kinds of crises which were intertwined. What sort of difference did Jesus make and who was he that he made that difference? And how does the community decide which are appropriate and adequate expressions of that difference? The answers to both these questions (the first, a question of *identity;* the second, the authority of certain *forms*) produced Catholicism.

EARLY CATHOLIC RESPONSES

For models of early Christian responses to the complicated questions of faith, we will focus upon some sharply etched representative documents and figures. There were beautiful Jewish-Christian texts like the *Didache* (about 60–117 C.E.), which described a Way of Light and a Way of Death, providing a Church order for its community (rules on fasting, prayer, baptism, the Eucharist, and how to deal with prophets, bishops, and deacons). Then there was Marcion (about 160) whose speculations about the God of Love present in Jesus forced him to reject the Hebrew Scriptures and their inferior Creator God. Marcion found that the Pauline letters supported his understanding of Christ's ransom from the fickle God's hold upon us; he also rejected all the Gospels but Luke's. He was successful enough that it became necessary to say which *were* the authentic texts upon which the community depended and in which it found its identity.

A Prophet

Justin Martyr (about 100–165 C.E.) began searching for God, as he related in his *Apology* (about 155), through pagan philosophies. The Stoics failed to tell him who God was; the Peripatetics said they would tell him, if he offered them money; the Pythagoreans wanted him to learn music, astronomy, and geometry first. Then Justin discovered the prophets and met the friends of Christ—and thus became a "true philosopher." Because Christians showed no fear in the face of violent death, Justin thought their religious posture must be worth investigation.

Taking the philosophical principle of the *Logos* (a rational and physical structure of cosmic order), Justin identified the fullness of this Reason with Christ.[1] The seed of the Logos was scattered in all human beings, making truthful pagans into Christians before their time. But Christ under his own rational power became the suffering servant, thus fulfilling the prophecies made about him. Justin had a principle (*Logos*) of continuity and discontinuity which he could apply to the Christian event. Moreover, the language of the Johannine Gospel about the Logos becoming flesh confirmed Justin's interpretations. Everyone shared rational words; only Christ Jesus himself was the complete word of the Godhead.

A Traditionist

Irenaeus of Lyons (about 130–200) attacked Gnosticism directly. He did so by stressing not a speculative system, but what could be called common sense. What was plainly visible, understandable, and audible was the rule of authentic interpretation. Christ was the recapitulation of all religious history, the coming to a head of God's utter love for the world.

Against Marcion, Irenaeus claimed only one God, creator and redeemer; against the Gnostics, he maintained both the goodness of the world and the origin of evil in human beings. Only an authentic Tradition and a creedal formula would protect the community from blatantly stupid formulations. So he appealed to his discipleship under Polycarp (about 69–155), the Bishop of Smyrna, who in turn was a pupil of John and "the rest of those who had seen the Lord." Heretics were the inventors of the new; what came from the original event through morally upright and community-approved leaders was authentic.

A Visionary

Besides Justin the prophet and Irenaeus the traditionist, there was also a visionary, whose writing, *The Shepherd of Hermas* (about 140–55), was ranked for many years with the Gospels and Letters of Paul. He received the vision of an elderly woman, the Church, who proclaimed that unless those who had fallen aside in recent prosperous times repented, they would be excluded from the coming Kingdom.

In the *Shepherd's* vision, the contemporary conscience of the Church unfolded. Neither entirely good nor evil, it needed a second plank of safety for the shipwrecked, a saving repentance from God after baptism. The author's perspective was that of an ordinary Christian, a freed slave who married, became a merchant, and lost his savings when his children denounced him during the recent persecution. Hoping against hope, he encouraged all God's children to return—no matter what their betrayals of the Master. But the time was short. God's future was breaking in.

THE TWO WAYS:
INTRINSIC AND EXTRINSIC RULES OF FAITH

It was precisely during the period of these three theologians—Irenaeus, Justin, and Hermas—that the church first identified its boundaries. Were the Gnostics really Christians? Are we so universal, so catholic, as to accept all understandings of the Christ-event? Can we reject the Hebrew Scriptures? On what grounds do we find our continuing identity in them? The answers given to these questions followed the two basic threads offered by Justin, Irenaeus, and Hermas: the authority of Apostolic Tradition and the ability of the Scriptures to explain both Christ *and* contemporary culture.

The canon, or rule of Scriptures, developed only slowly as an external norm for deciding what was an authentic Christian text and what was not. Justin Martyr was the first to appeal to written Christian texts, although others had quoted sayings and stories about Jesus. The ultimate authority of the religious book was that it reflected God's intentions for our world in Christ (2 Pet. 1:19–21). But it was only with the various collections of texts and their con-sequent community-founding authority that arguments could be made from them.

Eusebius (about 260–340), the historian and Bishop of Caesarea, provided a scriptural list approved by the Eastern Churches with which he was familiar. The Emperor Constantine (+337) used this catalog to offer fifty copies of the Bible to the Churches of Constan-tinople. This combination of ecclesial identity and political approval seems to have settled the matter, though it was Athanasius (about 296–373), the Bishop of Alexandria, and fighter for orthodoxy, who provided the final accurate listing in 367.

What seems like an arbitrary decision to limit the books which Christians could read during prayer and upon which they might reflect for moral and religious identity was not really capricious. Unified missionary efforts, internal instruction of those to be bap-tized, confusing interpretations of various factions, and finally perse-cution from secular authorities until the early fourth century forced upon the developing communities the need to determine their boundaries.

Although a variety of interpretations of Jesus was possible, not all could be sustained if the Tradition was to exist as a true unity. These approved texts became the foundational documents of the new Church. Their authority derived from a close connection with those who knew the Lord.

But there was always a requirement to see the external principle of authority as an internal event as well. The event of Jesus and the texts to which Justin appealed interpreted the culture in which he lived. There was an intrinsic principle through which God encountered the world, participated in it, and transformed it. The Christ-event was the true philosophy, the authentic Word to the world, not only because its texts came from an authentic past, but also because they could be found in the meaningful present.

Authority and measured cultural embodiment were the prophetic responses to the crises of early Christian identity. These two ways of governing and controlling the nest of images surrounding Jesus continue to be the main moments of Catholic religious life.

ORIGEN, FIRST SYSTEMATIC THEOLOGIAN

The most important attempt to achieve a coherent theological unity for Christianity in the early years was offered by Origen (about 185–254) in Alexandria. As the head of a school for catechumens (Christians preparing for baptism) and its primary instructor at an early age, he found it necessary to organize Christian theology in all areas. Consequently, his work fell into many categories. He determined accurate scriptural texts through the Hexapla or six-columned book which provided four translations of the Hebrew Scriptures. He wrote homilies and commentaries on all the Scriptures and composed the first treatise in systematic theology.

In *On First Principles* (220–30), Origen provided his synoptic vision of the universe with Christ as its center. These catechetical instructions, heavily influenced by his training in middle Platonic philosophy, investigated all reasonable opinions and provided consistent, clear arguments about the whole of Christian belief. Deeply conscious of the intellectual and moral weight Christ could have for the educated world, Origen mastered the range of scriptural data, organized available images and opinions, weighed conflicting interpretations, and constructed viable positions which he constantly revised.

The success of Origen's work can perhaps be seen by the fact that in the Eastern Churches, about every one hundred years after his death, there was a condemnation of one or another of his opinions. Origen preached, wrote, and taught at a time when Christian identity was still fluid. But he, above all, granted that his understanding of Christ was limited and that it could be corrected by further logic and Christian experience. In the end he believed that it was not knowledge but the power of God's grace enabling the will that saved us. "Mere clarity in stating the truth," he said, "will not suffice to move the human heart; words must be beautiful by grace."[2]

The prophets of early Christianity were those who spoke for unity: a unified interpretation of the past and a cogent understanding of the contemporary. They called for adherence to a Tradition which had emerged from Jesus and for a unity of intellectual, religious, and, ultimately, political culture which would protect and further the Christ-event.

THE NONBELIEVER'S REFUSAL: PLOTINUS

Their success may be seen in the response of the philosopher Plotinus (205–70 C.E.) who rejected Gnostic myths as well as the stories of Christian redemption. It was all so much confusing legend. Thought could lead to the Divine One; contemplation of Unity would bring personal and cosmic integration. Knowledge was not a matter of some blunt instrument handed to the spirit to travel back to Unity; rather it carefully criticized the options offered in our world, accepting or rejecting as occasion warranted.

But Plotinus's analyses, subtle, mystical, occasionally sublime, fell afoul of the problem of evil. For him evil in our world was a mere defect, a crack in the mirror of images we see, nothing for which we are particularly responsible, nothing which we can effectively overcome—except by philosophy. Samuel Taylor Coleridge reminded us well over a hundred years ago that philosophy would save only the few. Thought, critical and serious, is too difficult for the many; and the "most appropriate language of Religion" is imagination, the "poetic connection." What is needed is too awesomely important to be "trusted to the Stumblings and alternate Pro- and Re-gression of the growing Intellect of Man."[3]

Irenaeus, Justin, Hermas; the prophets, traditionists, and apocalyptic visionaries of Catholicism trusted to the unifying, transforming power of the Cross of Christ. Only that would make the world whole; only that would make the world one.

NOTES

1. *The Second Apology*, 2.10, in *Writings of St. Justin Martyr*, trans. Thomas B. Falls (New York: Christian Heritage, 1948), 129.
2. *Against Celsus*, chap. 6.2, as translated somewhat poetically in Jean Daniélou, *Origène* (Paris: Table Ronde, 1948), 112.
3. *The Philosophical Lectures of Samuel Taylor Coleridge*, ed. Kathleen Coburn (London: Pilot Press, 1949), 396.

FURTHER RELATED MATERIAL

For useful introductions to Semitic Christian thought forms, see the classic Jean Daniélou, *Theology of Jewish Christianity*, trans. John A. Baker (London: Darton, Longman & Todd, 1964) and his more general survey *Gospel Message and Hellenistic Culture*, trans. John A. Baker (Philadelphia: Westminster Press, 1973). For Gnosticism, see Robert Grant, *Gnosticism and Early Christianity* (New York: Columbia University Press, 1959) and Hans Jonas, *Gnostic Religion* (Boston: Beacon Press, 1963). For the entire period, see the analyses of Johannes Quasten, *Patrology*, 3 vols. (Utrecht-Antwerp: Spectrum, 1966—), Jaroslav Pelikan, *The Emergence of the Catholic Tradition* (Chicago: University of Chicago Press, 1972), and Robert M. Grant, *Early Christianity and Society* (New York: Harper & Row, 1977).

4

THE EMERGENCE OF
CATHOLIC CHRISTIANITY (III)
A Stable Social Reality

The banners of the king advance,
The mystery of the cross shines forth,
On which the founder of our flesh
Was suspended as from a gallows.

O blessed tree whose limbs
Supported the price of the planets!
O balance prepared to price the corpse,
You snatched the spoils from Sheol!
                Venantius Fortunatus (about 530–609),
                "Vexilla Regis Prodeunt."

The poet Venantius made his fortunate entry into what is now France in the late sixth century. Having completed a pilgrimage across the Alps to the shrine of Martin of Tours (+397, a bishop who had been proclaimed holy not by martyrdom but through a life of good deeds), he settled near Poitiers. He could not return to his own lands near Venice because the barbarian Lombards had invaded. Entering the service of Radegunde (518–87), the former wife of the Merovingian king Clothaire I (497–561), now a deaconess and foundress of a monastery of nuns, Venantius was first steward, then priest/chaplain of the community. Eventually he was elected bishop of Poitiers.

In 569, Radegunde received for her convent a portion of the Cross of Christ, found by Helen (about 255–330, the mother of the Emperor Constantine [+337]). Venantius composed a hymn ("The Banners of the King Advance") which has been part of Catholic worship ever since. Despite the barbarian incursions and the collapse of the remnants of imperial civilization, Venantius envisioned the once rejected Criminal's cross conquering the entire earth.

In the late sixth century, after the fall of the Roman Empire (476), it must have been difficult to believe that Jesus was Lord of the earth.

33

But in Venantius's own story there are the elements which, by the ninth century, would stabilize Western society into the new order which we now call Christendom. It was constructed from the hymns of poets like Venantius, the generosity of barbarian women like Radegunde, Roman familial government like Martin's, and the arbitrary military loyalties, oppositions, and religious sensibilities of various emperors, kings, and queens. In this cultural melting pot a new material was forged to support the religious quests of Catholic Christianity.

The Edict of Toleration (313 C.E.) agreed upon by the Eastern and Western emperors at Milan created a new situation for Christians. No longer would they be persecuted by governmental authorities. How would they take responsibility for their faith without a constantly hostile environment?

In this chapter we will describe some of the fundamental elements of Western Christianity: the earliest commentators on Scripture and society, known as the "Fathers" of the Church; the meetings, called synods and councils, held to sort out complicated cultural and religious questions; the development of unified symbols of worship; and the volcanic islands of monastic stability.

Each had to reflect upon serious issues.

Who belongs to this Christian movement?

What are the criteria for telling the difference between Gnostic, Jew, pagan, and Christian?

Is it a matter of the right doctrine (ortho-doxy) or of correct behavior (ortho-praxy)?

What are the rules for establishing unity within the community's diversity?

Will the rules developed in the second and third centuries (apostolic Tradition and theological principles of unity) be sufficient now that Christianity is an approved religion?

Venantius Fortunatus, like all the "antennae of our race" (Ezra Pound), anticipated that a successful, or at least an adequate, embodiment would be discovered.

THE FATHERS OF THE CHURCH: AUGUSTINE

In the earliest days of the Churches, it was clear who belonged. It was always those who were willing to lay down their lives (John

34

15:13–14) in martyrdom. So we have the official court proceedings against Justin (+165) and eyewitness accounts of Polycarp (+156) or Felicity and Perpetua, Africans condemned at Carthage (+203).

Ignatius of Antioch (+107), the Syrian bishop of Antioch, early successor to Peter, requested on his journey to Rome that his martyrdom not be stopped. He wished to be "ground by the teeth of wild beasts, that I may end as the pure bread of Christ."[1] Ignatius combined a severe Christocentric mysticism with uncompromising concentration of Church order as a way of re-presenting that authentic Christ. For this martyr that person was *catholicos,* that is, universal, catholic, who surrounded the bishop standing in the place of the Heavenly Father. The bishop was the responsible teacher, the unifier in truth, and the presider at worship.

It is this integration of religious interiority and external order that characterized the begetter of Western Catholicism, Augustine of Hippo (354–430). Without his concern for personal salvation from sin, his attempt to understand God's grace in individual life and universal history, his theology of Church and sacrament, his scriptural sermons and commentaries, there would have been no medieval Christendom and most assuredly no Reformation in the sixteenth century. With Augustine, we have a full exposition of the crucial relationship between institutional holiness and prophetic Church.

Unlike some of the more remote religious ancestors of our tradition, Augustine told his own story. His autobiographical classic, *The Confessions,* inaugurated an entire genre of literature: the introspective memoir which made unified sense of a lifetime's cultural and psychic change.

As a youth, Augustine tried whatever experience was available to an energetic North African male. Although he received a Christian familial upbringing, he drifted from it during his education in rhetoric at Carthage. There he took a mistress to whom he was faithful for fifteen years and by whom he fathered a child. He prayed: "Grant me chastity and continence, but not yet!"[2] He shifted his intellectual and personal interests successively toward Ciceronian philosophy, Manichaeism (a dualist Gnosticism), agnosticism, then Neoplatonism. He left northern Africa, traveled to Rome to open a school of rhetoric, departed there in anger, and located in Milan where he came under the influence of Ambrose, its bishop (about 339–97), who was known for his intelligence, holiness, and especially for his eloquent preaching. In all this he was unsatisfied. "Our hearts are restless till they find rest in Thee."[3]

His turn to God in Christ was swift and stunning. Though intellectually convinced of the religious value of Christian teaching, he was offended by its poor Latin; moreover he could not see the Christ beyond his moral blinders. In emotional and intellectual upheaval, Augustine sat in the garden of the house weeping. Overhearing children playing a game and calling to each other "Take and read; take and read," he opened the New Testament and his eyes fell upon this passage: "Let us behave with decency as befits the day: no revelling or drunkenness, no debauchery or vice, no quarrels or jealousies! Let Christ Jesus himself be the armor that you wear; give no more thought to satisfying the bodily appetites" (Rom. 13:13–14, NEB).

From that moment until his death, Augustine astonished the world: as bishop of Hippo he showed unusual skill and pastoral concern; as the first great synthetic Western theologian, he founded almost all areas of Western Christian philosophy and theology. This required not only an understanding of his own dreaded call to holiness, but also a vision of universal history under God's gracious assistance.

In the end, he says, one can dwell in only one of two cities: that of God, the way of charity and love of the Other for the Other's sake; or the city of human endeavor, a way of selfishness and self-seeking importance. Civil government, personal gain, and individual needs are valuable only insofar as they embody the City of God; otherwise they are merely sin. There can be no neutral acts in our lives.

Augustine spoke for the Pauline priority of God's love, his gracious assistance in human life. Whether it was in the controversy with the Donatists (a North African separatist group who argued that Christians who had lapsed during the persecutions should not be readmitted to communion) or with Pelagius and his followers (who stressed human ability to acquire virtue), Augustine argued for God's primary claim upon all reality. We are free because God has freed us; without Divine love, we would drift into sin. The sacramental life of the Church occurs because God acts in worship, not because we win Divine favor through our prayer.

In effect, both Donatists and Pelagians said that the public life of the Christian community (whether baptism or office) was human work, the achievement of men and women. If Christians were not inwardly holy, then the external actions of the community were void, without religious meaning. Augustine argued that the Church and its primary realizations, the sacraments, were the medium of God's activity. "The divine excellence abides in the sacrament, whether to the salvation of those who use it right, or to the destruction of those who use it wrong."[4]

The very holiness of God was mysteriously mediated through the historical, sacramental life of the Catholic community. "The Eucharist is our daily bread; but let us receive it in such a way, that we may be refreshed not in our bodies only, but in our souls. For the power which is apprehended there is unity, that gathered together into His body, and made His members, we may be what we receive. Then will it be indeed our daily bread."[5]

This mixture of interior conversion and external loyalty did not always cohere well in Augustine's understanding of Christianity. But it provided the vocabulary and the grammar of an entire age. He taught Western Christians to take the journey within—the search for God's Kingdom of truth inside themselves. From this, he constructed a theology which was willing even to probe the very mysterious Triune divinity itself.

Every great Christian renaissance—the twelfth–thirteenth centuries, the Reformation, even the contemporary existentialist revivals—has returned to Augustine as a prophetic model of how to reflect honestly and deliberately upon Christian life.

COUNCILS AND SYNODS: JUDGMENTS OF TRUTH

The meeting of Christian experience with the Greek and Roman world gave rise to a number of new and previously unexplored possibilities. Hellenistic Christians, confronted by their cultural heritage in philosophy, art, and science, questioned the Scriptures through logic, metaphysics, aesthetics, and physics.

We have noted how difficult it was for Augustine to accept the New Testament simply because of its poor Latin translations. He felt required to seek the interior message that was embodied in the inelegant style. Others besides Augustine were compelled to ask in what way the eternal, unchangeable, all-powerful Father could become flesh, limited, changing, and death-ridden. How was Jesus both divine and human simultaneously? These questions preoccupied Christians throughout the first six to eight centuries.

How did one reconcile the statements by Jesus which said: "I and the Father are one" (John 10:30, RSV), and the "Father is greater than I" (John 14:28 RSV)? Articulated judgments concerning the conflicts provoked by faith in Christ emerged in two stages which centered around the worldwide or Ecumenical Councils of Nicaea (325) and Chalcedon (451). The doctrinal and ecclesiastical decisions announced there constitute Catholic Tradition to the present day.

Schools of Interpretation

In the earliest Christian Churches there appeared two principal schools of thought about Christ which colored all intellectual and political discussions. The School of Antioch heard the Scriptures with a literal ear. Its reflections tended to follow Aristotle (384–322 B.C.E.) and to focus upon the historical nature of the text. Interpreters did not look for a hidden mystical meaning in the text, but for the sense intended by the author. As a result, they almost always emphasized the humanity of Jesus. In the controversies about the identity of Christ, they stressed the dual character of Jesus' Presence—his divinity and humanity—having little philosophical language available to disclose their unity.

The School at Alexandria, on the other hand, took its philosophical categories from Plato (427–347 B.C.E.) and Neoplatonic philosophers such as Plotinus (about 205–70 C.E.). In reading the Scriptures they stressed the allegorical, moral, and mystical meanings deep within the text. Above all, the believer had to recognize God's action in human history and his disclosure of himself in Jesus. This emphasis upon the divinity of Jesus tended to obscure his human experience, so that in more heterodox moments theologians like Apollinarius (310–90 C.E.) said that all the highest human faculties were simply replaced by divinity in Jesus. So just as Antiochenes stressed duality, Alexandrines preached unity and identity.

We do not need to rehearse the often difficult Greek philosophical, theological, and political debates of the period to see that crucial issues were at stake for Christian life. Beneath all the high words, the sometimes virulent attacks, the generous gestures, and the malicious deeds lay one question: Do the scriptural stories and theologies announce in Jesus salvation from death, sin, and failure? If Jesus was not divine in a human way, or human in a divine way, then our faith is in vain. The categories of these centuries were regularly metaphysical and philosophical; the issue was existential reconciliation or separation from God.

Putting the Question: Arius and Apollinarius

Arius (about 250–336) formulated the question so sharply in Alexandria that no one could ignore it. For him, the Logos who became flesh (John 1:14) was a creature, a better than human but not quite completely divine being. Arius's interpretation succeeded, not only because of his personal asceticism, popular preaching ability, and political connections, but because it seemed utterly logical. To be both human and divine required a bit of both mixed together. In this way, God could still remain sovereignly free, unchanging, and eternal while humanity maintained its qualitative difference as limited, sinful, and historical.

Apollinarius, Bishop of Laodicea (about 310–90), was an ardent anti-Arian. He proclaimed the divinity of Christ without qualification. There was certainly no moral development in Christ. Humanity and divinity were united in him. Therefore Apollinarius argued that although Christ had a human body and soul, he had only a Divine Spirit, the Spirit of the Word. This argument against Arius was disastrous. For if Christ was not completely human, then how could he be a true example for us? How would he have redeemed all of our human reality?

Athanasius and Conciliar Judgments

The great figures of the Eastern theological Tradition, such as Athanasius (about 296–373), argued otherwise. For him, Jesus was both fully human and fully divine—however philosophically illogical that might seem. But how can One who is unbounded be born in a womb? How can one who is so sincerely human—compassionate, crying, eating, and drinking—be divine *precisely in* that humanity?

For Catholic Christians these issues were articulated into official

39

positions called doctrines between 325 and 681. The two principal councils were the first and fourth of six. Called by the Emperor Constantine, the Council of Nicaea (325) solemnly declared that the true belief of Christians was that Jesus Christ as Son of God was equal to (of the same substance—or in Greek, *homoousios* with) God the Father and Holy Spirit. The Christian God was One and Triune simultaneously. At Constantinople (381), further clarification concerning the Holy Spirit was added; and it fathered the Nicene-Constantinopolitan Creed (the so-called Nicene Creed) which is prayed by Catholics each Sunday. The fourth ecumenical council, Chalcedon (451), declared that Jesus Christ was truly human and truly divine, that the one person of Christ existed in two natures.

Neither doctrine stopped theological discussion; indeed, if anything, they pushed it forward. They provided a non-Scriptural language which re-presented to Greek (and Latin) culture the same message as the New Testament. Repeating the New Testament stories did not solve the question Arius asked; finding a new set of words in which to proclaim Christ to another culture did.

Mind had asked a question: "Is he or is he not a creature?" Reason deserved a religious answer commensurate with its intelligence. Jesus was a part of our real world; so was his salvation. It had either made a difference to that one world or it had not. The Councils maintained that Catholic Christians could not retreat to a private religious world to nurse their personal symbols, nor could they be parents of some divergent logic which operated in religion and not in the world at large. However hard it might be, the Christian would be required to find an adequate embodiment of Christian faith in the articulated beliefs of particular ages.

WORSHIP: THE PLACE OF BELIEF

The familiar Catholic blessing "In the name of the Father and of the Son and of the Holy Spirit" and the gestures of touching the forehead, the chest, and shoulders symbolize something very important. For just as surely as they announce the central belief of Trinitarian experience, they are also worship, the experience of prayer. The doctrines of Catholic Christianity, whether intellectual or ecclesiastical, were born in address to the Father of the living Jesus.

Prosper Tiro of Acquitaine (about 390–463) canonized this important ecclesial principle. "The law of worship establishes the law of belief."[6] In the reports of the major Councils we have just mentioned, this was most certainly the case. The Fathers of the Councils appealed at Nicaea to the baptismal liturgy to justify their expression of Trinitarian faith. It was because the community baptized through triple immersion in the name of Father, Son, and Spirit that the Creed confessed God as triune. At Chalcedon it was the simple fact that Christians prayed *to* Christ as well as *through* him that convinced the bishops and theologians that Jesus could be confessed as both divine and human. We would not blasphemously worship a creature.

The sacramental life of the Christian community was a way in which it was catholic. The common gestures, the common Gospels proclaimed at worship, the eating and drinking in memory of the Lord Jesus defined Christians throughout the empire, despite cultural, gestural, or linguistic differences. So Pliny (62–113), the governor of Bithynia (northwest Asia Minor), wishing to confirm his persecution of Christians, wrote about their gathering at dawn before the workday to worship.

In early years both the one who presided and the prayers said at the main service of worship differed from place to place. But by the mid-second century (for example, in Justin Martyr), there was considerable structural analogy from one Church to another both in order of worship and the leaders of prayer. The combination of readings from the New Testament, prayers for the living and the dead, acceptance of gifts (both bread and wine or food and monetary offerings for the poor), the great thanksgiving prayer including the memorial of the Lord's final supper, a common "Our Father," and the breaking and distribution of the sacred Bread and Wine to those present were all constants in both Eastern and Western liturgies of the Eucharist (after *Eucharistia*, the Greek word for thanksgiving). Such communion was a sharing in the Body of Christ, as Augustine had stated.

But the Body of Christ has many members (1 Cor. 12:12–31), not all of whom accomplish the same tasks. St. Paul's images and the growth of the community prompted individual Churches to adopt an organization which would pattern their experience of worship and culture. Catholics modeled their ecclesiastical experience more and more upon a stratified civil government. With the acceptance of Christianity as a legitimate religion of the empire, the local "over-seer" or bishop assumed not only the role of chief presider at worship and authentic interpreter of doctrinal discussions, but became a sign and hierarchical bond of political unity as well. As it became more and more difficult for the local bishop to preside over worship in outlying districts, he appointed priests, that is, presbyters, to take his place. The common gesture of inauguration for such specialized ministries in the Church was the laying on of hands.

Both belief and Church order emerged from worship. The need to clarify the symbolic expressions of the community issued in the Councils and creeds. The requirement to structure social prayer created normative offices in the community. These Hellenistic de-velopments of doctrine are particularly Catholic. Such reformula-tions make utterly clear that the Catholic Tradition is an organic history, adapting to new situations without losing its roots in the original experience of Christ. The type of its identity is preserved, even if the form changes.

The intensely personal preaching and theology of Augustine and other fathers, the development of a canon of authentic scriptural texts, the discernment of right teaching in the doctrines of councils, and the achievement of structurally analogous forms of worship and Church order provided the marks of the Catholic Church at the conclusion of the sixth century when Venantius Fortunatus made his pilgrimage to Gaul. There was a recognizably universal community of believers which had grappled creatively with the dying culture and attempted to transform it through an extraordinary program of personal and societal evangelization. To sustain its identity, Chris-tianity asserted itself as part of an edifice of classical life whose achievements it recognized, whose sins it deplored, and whose politi-cal government it used to spread the Gospel. The story of Jesus was becoming the foundation stone of an entire civilization.

But in the fifth and sixth centuries, the old Roman traditions were collapsing. Christians were taking control of various political offices because the old apparatus at the edges of the empire was disintegrat-ing. Before we can understand that distinctively Catholic culture called medieval Christendom, we must examine an important prophetic movement. It is a place where the tradition of texts, the prophetic missionary, and the proclamation of the apocalyptic Heavenly Jerusalem met—the movement called monasticism.

THE PROPHETS OF EARLY MONASTICISM

Every religious impulse has its ascetic or rigorist movements. So there are solitary hermits in Buddhism and Hinduism, philosophical ascetics such as Pythagoras (about 570–496 B.C.E.), and the Essenes (about 100 B.C.E.–200 C.E.) in Judaism. The origin of Christian ascetic movements seems to have been in Egypt where solitaries (called in Greek *monachos,* monks) went to the deserts in their quest for religious unification, coherence, and integrity. From earliest days, such hermits lived celibate lives. Following Paul's dictum that it was better not to marry due to the coming Day of the Lord (1 Cor. 7:25–40), monks struggled for an undivided heart, for simplicity of spirit in anticipation of the Parousia (the glorious return of Christ).

With the persecutions of the Emperor Decius (250–51), the crisis in the fervor of the Christian community became acute. Monasticism spread in response as an escape from lax or lapsed believers in urban areas and as an attempt to recover the original dedication of Christian missionaries, martyrs, and apostles.

In the *Life of Antony* (about 251–356), Athanasius (about 296–373) praises this Egyptian ascetic who gave away his goods and property in addition to his right to marry. The holiness of Antony's hermitlike life attracted followers who gathered around him in an ordered community of work and prayer.

Pachomius (about 290–346), a former soldier, founded a monastery at Tabennisi in the Thebaid near the Nile about 320. He developed an austere rule for his community; yet before he died, he ruled as *abbas* (abbot) over nine foundations of men and women. He believed that his coenobitic (i.e., communitarian) monasticism recovered the "apostolic life" of the early Christian community (Acts 4:42–47) in which prayer, property, and possessions were ideally held in common.

Basil the Great (about 330–79) provided the common rule for most urban monastic foundations in the Eastern Empire. The rule of charity was paramount. As he said: "If you live alone, whose feet will you wash?" While strict poverty, chastity, and obedience to an abbot were required, hours of liturgical prayer, manual labor, and even the education of children in schools attached to the monasteries were encouraged. The poor were always to be welcomed. This communitarian experience disclosed the presence of the Heavenly City on earth.

By the early fifth century there were so many Latin Christians in Eastern monasteries that it became necessary to provide a rule in their vernacular. An Eastern monk, John Cassian (about 360–435), brought Egyptian monasticism to the West near Marseilles. Out of his years in the East he wrote *The Institutes* and *Conferences,* which record the ordinary rules of community life and the various hindrances to perfection.

Benedict of Nursia (about 480–550) retired to a cave at Subiaco in Italy, but as a hermit he attracted religious disciples who eventually founded a monastic community at Monte Cassino (about 525). The *Rule of St. Benedict,* which draws from Cassian, Basil, the desert monks, and Augustine, but especially from the New Testament, provided a prudent, humane, common life. He wished to found a "school of the Lord's service." This has become through the centuries the charter document of all later monastic experience in the Western Catholic Church.

THE CATHOLIC COMMUNITY

The influence of monastic life in the Church cannot be neglected. Its emphasis upon simplicity, self-discipline, and the meditative reading of the Scriptures and the Fathers plus a strong centralized government around an abbot inaugurated an extraordinary gesture of stability in the chaotic Western world. The radical demands of the cross and resurrection had met the need to remain within one's social environment in a holy way.

In the early Church, martyrdom was an obvious sign of membership in the definitive religious community. Now the struggle to develop concrete incarnations of holiness in an empire which permitted and even encouraged Christianity had become the Church's most important task. The early prophetic and even apocalyptic strains of the Christ-event kept solidifying into Tradition and custom. How was this original event to be kept authentic?

The early conflicts of the believing community through their resolutions in doctrine, creed, office, sacraments, Councils, and most of all through their creative theologians, provided evidence of the electricity transmitted in Jesus of Nazareth. In a sense, if the prophetic character of the event had *not* become Tradition in a series of religious institutions, it would not only have died; it would have given evidence simply of its ultimate bankruptcy as a religious enterprise.

The early Church was not simply a *gnosis,* a knowledge or a speculative theology. To be Catholic, to be faithful to the radiance of that astonishing Jesus, Christians were forced to examine not only the limits of the intellectual interpretations of its message, but also the practical, quite ordinary implications of holiness. For creeds, doctrines, and theologies were only one side of the ecclesial reality. Sacrament, the offices of bishop, priest, deacon, and deaconess were the social embodiment of the interior horizon envisioned by all believers.

Monasticism is a fruitful place to conclude this brief description of the marks of Catholic Christianity. The monks and women religious of East and West were utterly seminal in the stabilization of the interior, as well as exterior, elements in the Church. Their fundamental thrust toward the interiorization of the Christian message, coupled with the sacramental, liturgical, and governmental externals, made them a magnetic force in evangelization. And although the tensions between the visible and invisible aspects of Catholic existence have remained throughout its history, no one can refuse to see in this central institutional expression elements of prophetic proclamation, apocalyptic withdrawal, and purification encapsulated in a Tradition of prayerful meditation and cultural preservation. The dangerous memory of Jesus of Nazareth—his table fellowship with the poor and the outcast, his disclosure of God's gracious love—was being transmitted to the future.

NOTES

1. Letter to the Romans 1.2, 2.1, 4.1, in *The Apostolic Fathers,* trans. Francis X. Glimm, Joseph Marique, Gerald G. Walsh (New York: Christian Heritage, 1947), 108.
2. *Confessions of St. Augustine,* VIII.7, trans. J. G. Pilkington, in *Nicene*

and Post-Nicene Fathers, ed. Philip Schaff (New York: Charles Scribner's Sons, 1902), 124.

3. Ibid., I.1, p. 45.

4. On Baptism against the Donatists, see III.10.15, in *Writings in Connection with the Donatist Controversy,* trans. J. R. King (Edinburgh: T. & T. Clark, 1872), 62.

5. Sermon VII on Matthew 6, in *Nicene and Post-Nicene Fathers,* VI:282.

6. *Indiculus,* chap. 8 in *The Teaching of the Catholic Church,* ed. Josef Neuner, Heinrich Roos, and Karl Rahner (Staten Island, N.Y.: Alba House, 1966), 376.

FURTHER RELATED MATERIAL

There are three fine books on St. Augustine among the many: Peter Brown, *Augustine of Hippo: A Biography* (Berkeley and Los Angeles: University of California Press, 1967); Eugene Teselle, *Augustine the Theologian* (London: Burns & Oates, 1970); and G. Van der Meer, *Augustine the Bishop* (New York: Harper & Row, 1965). For conciliar history, see G. L. Prestige, *God in Patristic Thought* (London: SPCK, 1969); for a theory of what was going forward during the period, see B. J. F. Lonergan, *The Way to Nicea: The Dialectical Development of Trinitarian Theology* (Philadelphia: Westminster Press, 1976). On the developments in worship, Gregory Dix's *The Shape of the Liturgy* (London: A. & C. Black, 1970); and on monasticism, Helen Waddell, *The Desert Fathers* (Chicago: University of Chicago Press, 1958); or better, but less available, Derwas J. Chitty, *The Desert a City* (Oxford: Basil Blackwell & Mott, 1966) and Lowrie J. Daly, *Benedictine Monasticism: Its Formation and Development through the Twelfth Century* (New York: Sheed & Ward, 1965), and the historical introduction to *RB 1980: The Rule of St. Benedict,* ed. Timothy Fry (Collegeville, Minnesota: Liturgical Press, 1981), especially 3–151.

THE TAMING OF EUROPE (692–1073)

> Franks, Romans and all believers
>   are immersed in misery and great distress.
>   O my sorrow!
> Infants, the old, grand prelates, and mothers
>   weep at the loss of Caesar.
>   O my sorrow!
> Never shall the rivers of tears cease,
>   for the whole world laments the death of Charles.
>   O my sorrow!
> Common Father to all: orphans and widows,
>   wanderers and maidens.
>   O my sorrow!
> Christ, you who govern the armies of the skies,
>   In your kingdom grant rest to Charles.
>   anon., from *A Solis Ortu* (800–900)

There is a capital sculpture in the eleventh-century atrium of the church at Saint-Benoît-sur-Loire in which two large creatures vie for control over a doll-like figure suspended between them. The being on the left is scaly of face, swathed in flaming skins, with a bloated countenance perched on a heavy body, legs planted firmly on the pillar below. His leechlike mouth remains eternally open, prepared to suck in whatever might feed his master's appetite, while his eyes stare resolutely toward the earth. Hovering over the pillar the seraph on the right enfolds his invisible torso in neatly pleated drapery which repeats the pattern of his wings. His face is long and narrow, crowned with Roman curls, jeweled with wide eyes directed toward the heavens. His mouth smiles. In between lies poor humanity. Blank-eyed, staring eternally forward, neither right nor left, up nor down, the figure is naked, distended in the arms by the tension of enormous powers beyond his control. He is caught—and the centuries have taken away his mouth. Is the creature screaming in terror at its predicament or comforted, knowing that the angel has cupped his right hand in blessing over its head?

Struggle may be the operative word for the early Middle Ages and its Church. Human ambiguity and the paradox of experience sometimes seemed overwhelming. And if the Catholic Church had found the basic instruments of religious cultivation in its doctrines, creeds, ordinations, and sacraments, the fields in which it tilled regularly resisted or grew strange hybrids which eventually required serious weeding.

AN OVERVIEW—THE PAINS OF GROWTH

This period (692–1073) begins with strife between the Eastern and Western branches of the Church and ends with two churches and a war between ecclesiastical and civil society in the West. At the Council called Quinisext (692), East and West diverged over largely disciplinary matters (such as celibacy for the clergy, the Lenten fast, and the primacy of Constantinople or Rome). Religious and civil politics occasionally divided the churches governed from the seats of the Eastern and Western Empires through 1054, when the two episcopal sees condemned each other.

This breach between Greek-speaking and Latin-speaking Catholicism formed the Greek Orthodox family of Churches. The excommunications (prohibiting intercommunion among Churches along with other legal consequences) were lifted only in 1965 when Pope Paul VI and the Patriarch Athenagoras embraced in Jerusalem.

In 1073 Hildebrand (about 1021–85) was elected as Pope Gregory VII. Convinced of the West's need for internal moral reform, he attempted to extricate the secular from the religious duties of Catholicism. Papal government was centralized and augmented. The High Middle Ages, to be assessed in the next chapter, had begun.

The world of early medieval Catholicism was confused. There were further invasions into the old boundaries of the Western Empire. Islam and Constantinople both had more sophisticated levels of culture. Moreover, the population of the West was thin, growing only slowly until about 1300; nonetheless, agriculture continued to lag behind the enlarging market for goods and food until the early 1200s. Multiple local lords claimed property, the only stable currency. In the midst of this stood the Church, claiming allegiance to a Lord whose rule was meant to extend over all powers and over all commercial goods. How was this community of believers to assert the transcendent goal *within* the early medieval experience? It chose social order and religious law.

With the assistance of certain spectacularly successful princes, the Church struggled for its catholicity by contributing to the building of a stratified ecclesial and secular society. This social order is known as *feudalism,* a system of allegiances originally meant to stop petty wars and vicious vendettas. Sometimes it succeeded; often it failed— allowing the Church to slip itself into the arsenal of princes or prelates who were quite willing to use divine legitimation for their own personal gain.

But we must begin where we earlier concluded—with monasticism. As the world approached the end of the first millennium, its theme was order and unity—which could too easily translate into servile obedience to one's superiors and a uniformity of expression.

MONASTIC MISSIONARIES— THE PROPHETS TO PEOPLES

Monks may have wanted to establish a permanent Heavenly City on earth; but within one hundred years of Benedict's major foundations, Irish and English missionaries were making pilgrimages from their communities to evangelize the barbarian continent. Celtic missionaries like Columbanus (about 543–615) and Gall (550–645) planted islands of stability among the barbarians of Gaul, Switzerland, and Italy. These austere missionaries brought with them a love of learning and the desire for God.[1] The schools of writing and textual preservation at St. Gallen, Bobbio, and Luxeuil founded some of the most famous continuing libraries in Europe.

Boniface, Apostle of Unity

The Celtic Church in England had been largely destroyed by the Saxon invasions during the fifth century. Yet rapidly, Saxon monks like Willibrord (658–739), a native of Northumbria, followed the same paths as their Celtic forebears.

The greatest of these missionaries was Boniface (680–754), or Wynfrith as he was originally known. Unsuccessful in Frisia, he went to Rome where he was given papal authority to preach in Germany.

His courage in chopping down the oak dedicated to Thor transformed him into an invincible hero. Here was no weak word-man, but an engaging, muscular personality, absolutely dedicated to the single cause of preaching the Gospel of Christ. His mission was to found bishoprics and monasteries in Germany, to establish settled ecclesiastical points from which the Church could radiate its catholicity.

Boniface combined in himself Latin and barbarian cultures and offered a clear identity to his converting Christians. He searched for intercultural answers to the problems of relatives' marriages, the validity of sacramental life performed by false, heretical, or even evil priests, and the social order of government and Church.

His solutions were important. "It is our earnest desire to maintain the Catholic faith and the unity of the Roman Church. As many hearers or learners as God shall grant me in my missionary work, I will not cease to summon and urge them to render obedience to the Apostolic See."[2] Boniface, through cultural training and religious conviction, evangelized the Saxons with Roman art, language, literature, and traditions. To overcome the fragmentation which he saw among the barbarians and to establish the Gospel, he implanted uniform doctrines and morals.

One and the same faith was always believed everywhere, as Vincent of Lérins (+ about 450) said. Christianity was identical from the beginning, and what better place to find the origin of that unity than in Rome where Peter and Paul were martyred? Boniface's extraordinary success at establishing ecclesiastical provinces served only to prove the point. Barbarians were interested in the civilizing influence of the Roman Church.

The Apostles of the East

This interpretation is born out in noticing, by way of contrast, the two great missionary brothers to eastern Europe, Cyril (+869) and Methodius (+885). They translated the Scriptures and liturgies into early Slavonic, inventing an alphabet for the purpose (Cyrillic). Although Cyril is buried in the Roman Church of San Clemente, Latinizing missionaries north of the Alps were not at all pleased with their efforts, so much so that at one point Methodius was imprisoned by German bishops for two years. Nonetheless, Slavonic continued to foster not a Latinized barbarian culture, but a vernacular expression of Christian Greek culture. It was this Christian culture which spread in the tenth century to the lands governed by the Rus.

These missionary efforts would have been fruitless without military and governmental support. An instance of this can be seen in the Arab incursions across the Pyrenees as far north as the Loire River just south of Paris. In 732, Charles Martel (about 690–741) defeated the Saracens at Poitiers in pitched battle. Without the peace created by the empire and an unqualified allegiance to it, Boniface's attempts to frame laws and provinces for the Church would have been in vain.

The Public Consequence of Sin

Public law and evangelical precept met in the Christian experience of sin. For despite the fact that the monastic missionaries wished to be absolutely faithful to the practice of the Roman Church, they introduced into the continent a private form of penance. Since *Hermas* it had been possible to have a second chance after baptism, but in a purely public fashion, by joining the ranks of penitents— wearing special garb, separating oneself from other Christians, and living a thoroughly ascetic life until death. Before the fourth century some sins were for all practical purposes "unforgivable" (apostasy, adultery, and murder).

Celtic and English Evangelizers brought with them the monastic practice of constant examination of conscience and the confession of faults to one's religious brothers. They enshrined this penitential practice in books of tariff penances which informed the priest what to impose upon the lax Christian. For example, for a monk, drunkenness required 30 days of penance, while for a priest or deacon, 40 days. Fornication with a virgin brought one year of strict penitential discipline; but intercourse with a married woman required four years. There were even penances for theft, murder, and heresy— sometimes up to twenty years of penance.[3]

What became important in this civilization of barbarian society was that religious actions had real consequences in the world. One was separated by fasting, habits of marital abstinence, and prayerful practices from those one knew and loved. Penance became compatible with certain forms of barbarian law in which one must "pay back" one's harm to another by a reparation fee (*wergeld*). If one sinned, one paid a spiritual restoration.

Later it became possible to ameliorate or even cancel penance through a financial gift which mandated prayers said at a particular monastery. Wealthy (or particularly military) princes began to found monasteries *before* they went out to do battle, just in the event that they might offend in some religious fashion. Society was beginning to fuse into unity—but not always to the benefit of the Gospel's confrontation of human values.

THE CONSOLIDATION OF TRADITION: SOCIETY AND CHURCH

The Carolingian Renaissance

King of the Franks and the Lombards, first ruler of the Holy Roman Empire, Charlemagne (742–814) governed both Church and state with grace, intelligence, and power. When he died, many looked at the Carolingian Renaissance of culture and governmental solidity as the ideal. The cathedral at Aachen, built between 796 and 804, modeled Ravennese mosaics for the northern kingdoms. Its octagonal dome towered over the countryside; God and king were praised together under the magnificent circular lights suspended from its center.

By title, of course, Charlemagne was only ruler of the state. But in his various capitularies (church regulation issued as civil laws) he centralized the patterns for ecclesiastical reform. The General Admonition of 798 mandated a school for every cathedral Church, annual visitation of bishops to the Churches of their dioceses (in conjunction with a civil governor to ensure that the bishop did his duty), a standardized religious instruction for all the baptized, the imposition of the Rule of Benedict upon monasteries in the kingdom, and tithes to be given to the Church. Charlemagne appointed almost all bishops and abbots directly and regularly disposed of ecclesiastical property as though it were the crown's. By various synods of bishops, he was described as the "devoted defender of holy Church" (Capitulary of 769), God's official, the Lord of the Church in the kingdom, the rector of the Church, priest, and king. In his circle of intimates, where classical nicknames prevailed, he was known as David the King.

After Charlemagne had stabilized the Italian political situation and confirmed Leo III (795–816) in his election, the pope crowned him Roman Emperor, Augustus (800). The pope then knelt and offered him homage, separating himself from his Byzantine loyalties. This gesture of the pope's severed Charlemagne's political ties with the Eastern Empire for some time; only in 812 did the Greek Emperor recognize this German as Emperor of the Western Empire.

Papal and Imperial Politics

Within one hundred years of Charlemagne's death, however, a synod of bishops near Laon (909) announced: "The world is full of lechery and adultery, churches are robbed and the poor are oppressed and murdered." As Church and state marched toward the end of the first millennium, they found themselves locked in a struggle of imperial proportions. For just as the classical culture of Rome believed there was really only one culture, normative for all times and places; so too its inheritors, whether Church or state, were convinced that only one institutional tradition could be supreme. Thus in the same fashion that Charlemagne consolidated political power, ecclesiastical powers attempted unification of Church under the government of Rome.

The regularly confused politics of Italy constantly encouraged papal-imperial confrontations. By mid-eighth century, there was a developing papal duchy surrounding Rome. At the same time, the last Merovingian king of the Franks was interned in a monastery; and Pepin the Short (714–68) took an oath (754) to protect the pope against the Lombards in the North.

A document, originating in the Frankish church and called the "Donation of Constantine," appeared, purporting to give the pope primacy over the major sees of the East (Antioch, Constantinople, Alexandria, and Jerusalem) and dominion over Italy. Within 100 years the text found its way into the Pseudo-Isidorean Decretals compiled near Le Mans or Tours. These collections of canons, letters, and laws were largely forgeries; but during the entire Middle Ages they were thought to be genuine both by proponents and opponents of papal hegemony.

Despite the attempts to make ecclesiastical life orderly, there were bizarre moments. The mid-ninth to the mid-tenth century is known by historians as the "obscure age" of papal history. One macabre example will suffice. Various successors to Charlemagne's children claimed Italian political loyalties. Pope Formosus (891–96) granted the imperial crown to a count of Spoleto of French lineage. He and his son's oppressive rule prompted the pope to ask the German king to establish order in Italy. The German king responded, took Rome, and received the imperial throne, but was stricken by paralysis before he could control the city and provinces. His seven-year-old son reigned briefly (900–911). Formosus's successor as pope held office for only two weeks; the next pope, Stephen VI (896–97), an enemy of the Franks, had the body of Formosus disinterred, stripped, and mutilated at a synod. He passed judgment upon the corpse as invalidly elected, annulling all the laws and orders conferred by him. Stephen was strangled in prison during an uprising; two years later his synodal laws against Formosus were repealed. The incident speaks for itself.

Only with the rise of the Ottonian dynasty (936–1000) in Germany did the Church begin to forge some independence from local Italian politics. Bishops and abbots became princes of the imperial realm, more able by their civil status to wrest independence from local lords and landowners. Monastic foundations were exempted from local taxation and made subject to the pope himself, thus giving them important leverage in the struggle for free expression of the Gospel.

Beautiful Letters

These centuries are murky, "dark" in many ways. Yet while the larger civil and ecclesiastical conflicts were engaged, monks were quietly preserving antiquity's religious and secular manuscripts. Without their excruciating effort, we would have no access to classical culture. Barrel-vaulted churches with Romanesque arches were constructed, solving serious architectural problems. The schools Charlemagne founded under Alcuin of York's (735–804) tutelage diminished clerical illiteracy and fostered a literary language with an accurate scribal orthography.

Extraordinary religious poetry in the vernacular, such as the Old English *Dream of the Rood* (about 750) or the Old Saxon *Heliand*

(*Savior*, about 800), was composed describing Christ as the primary prince to whom we owe allegiance and the apostles as his faithful vassals. Going against the grain, they counsel humility as virtue in the authentic Lord and love for one's enemies. During the same period monastic foundations such as Gandersheim (Saxony) or Nivelles (Belgium) increased, offering women access to educational emancipation. Biblical commentaries were fostered by theological controversies of the period ultimately culminating in a *General Commentary* (or *Glossa Ordinaria*) on the entire Bible which could be used as a basic textbook for lectures in the schools.

The Heroes of Memory

Three important thinkers of this period consolidate an important element in medieval life. The philosopher Boethius (about 480–524) translated and commented upon Aristotle's works on logic and grammar, wrote a brief theological work on the Trinity, and described in *On the Consolation of Philosophy* the way of the human soul to wisdom. Written in prison, this book converted many Western religious to the way of philosophy as well as to Christianity.

Bede the Venerable (about 673–735), a Northumbrian monk, is the Father of English Church history. His *Ecclesiastical History of the English People* evidences his genius as a historian, gathering information from firsthand witnesses when possible, weighing authorities, and sorting likely from unlikely events.

John Scotus Eriugena (about 810–77), in a treatise on nature, attempted to reconcile Neoplatonic physical cosmology with Christian creationism. His belief in the unity of the Genesis accounts and classical culture is shown in his translations of the mystical writings which went under the name of Dionysius. These works stressed the union of the Christian soul with God in wordless and imageless wonder and affected all later religious thought and liturgical practice.

Each of these thinkers patterns perhaps *the* important trait of medieval thought—the security of having reflected previous Tradition. Bede, Boethius, and Eriugena quote authorities, whether philosophical or religious, to prove their point. Their greatest horror in many ways was to be "new," original, separated from the Tradition from which they emerged. Despite their own considerable abilities at synthesis, they preferred to think of themselves as craftsmen, carefully tooling already tried materials into excellent shapes and designs. From the debris of cultural and political morals, religion, and statecraft, they hoped to preserve the truth from the transient errors of the present in much the same way that their contemporaries shaped gilded shrines for the bones or relics of holy men and women of the past. Without this connection with days gone by, one was lost. The thinkers' careful retention of antique polished jewels helped restore faith in a future which seemed confused and offered some glimmer of hope in their present.

THE CRISIS OF THE FUTURE: THE COMING OF THE MILLENNIUM

Crisis produces apocalyptic writings. It is no surprise that the struggles for power and identity in the early Middle Ages called upon that critical New Testament grammar of religious possibilities. Surely the victorious Son of Man would return to cleanse his community of the buyers of ecclesiastical offices, murderers of the innocent, and knightly despoilers of the countryside.

The medieval figures whom we must briefly mention could not ignore the perilous times. They criticized their contemporaries in the light of God's universal plan for history. The conversion of the Roman Empire, the invasions of Islam, the developing centralized papacy, the closure of one thousand years of Christian history—each provided a nodal point around which visions clustered. While philosophy dealt with the universal eternal laws of time and space and the institutional traditions focused upon preserving the past, apocalyptic writing of the period offered believers and thinkers a way of locating the specific events and cultural shifts of the present within a history directed by God's victorious justice and liberating love.

Papal Foreclosure

Curiously enough we may begin with Pope Gregory I (590–604). Son of a senator, he sold his property, becoming first a monk, then a deacon of Rome, diplomat to Constantinople, and pope. He fostered liturgical reform, including support of the music known as plainsong or Gregorian chant. Gregory was a masterful preacher and spiritual guide. His pastoral rule for bishops became a handbook; his commentary on Job a mine of practical moral judgments and ethical theory. As administrator, he challenged barbarians and emperors and sent missionaries to England.

But amid all this remarkable constructive activity, Gregory believed that society had little future. "Cities are destroyed, armed camps overturned, districts emptied of people, the earth reduced to solitude. . . . Let us despise with all our being this present—or rather extinct—world."[4] Gregory was convinced that the terrors of the present—climatic changes, wars, famines—were signs of the times, the presage of the judgment of God.

Cultural Confrontations

The Eastern Empire shared this pessimistic vision. A seventh-century Syrian author (Pseudo-Methodius of Patara) anticipated a last world emperor who would vanquish the invading Moslems. There was to be no collaboration with these children of Ishmael and no reliance upon weak rulers for assistance. Only God would suffice.

Where culture clashed with culture, schemes of eschatological conflict flourished. In an Old High German relic of the ninth century, Elijah meets the Antichrist, that mysterious figure (with origins in 2 Thess. 2:6–7) who would appear before the End to torture the earth. Elijah's wounds in this battle would make the mountains catch fire, destroy the trees, and dry up the waters. Even the bonds of tribe and nation would break down.

Abbot Adso (910–92) shifted the scene of the final warfare between good and evil from either Constantinople or Rome. The conquering emperor, the one in whom we hope for victory over the Antichrist, would be the king of the Franks. After terrifying trials this ruler would govern Christ's empire, travel to Jerusalem, and put aside his scepter and crown on the Mount of Olives. The Antichrist would be killed by the humble power of the Lord Jesus alone. The time for this judgment is the present.

CONCLUSIONS

These negative visions of the world gained inflated currency as the millennium approached. Abbo of Fleury (about 945–1004) remarked that he had heard a sermon as a young man which proclaimed that "as soon as the number of a thousand years was completed, the Antichrist would come and the Last Judgment would follow. I opposed this sermon with what force I could."[5] But rumor continued to thrive. What is one to make of these developments? Are they in some way religious? How are they Catholic?

The pain of religious incarnation in various cultures is acute. It is not accomplished without false starts, blind alleys, and the corridors of power. The early Middle Ages knew only one normative society, the decaying Roman Empire, a government in which religion supported the state and state was founded upon religious ritual, order, and narrative. The struggles between Church and empire upon which we now look with somewhat bemused or belligerent antipathy for their seeming venality, collusion, and neglect of the Gospel may in fact reflect something more important.

For without the attempts by the Church to establish itself as an independent political enterprise, it might have been swallowed completely by the maw of the state. Papal and episcopal politics were regularly an attempt to maintain maneuverability within an increasingly narrowed situation. While that does not condone evil, it helps explain some history. Church without property in early feudal society was a Gospel without independence. It became a court jester, supporting the prince in good or bad policy, telling only occasional ironic tales to tweak the conscience of the powerful. And though this was sometimes the case during this period (and others we shall study), even spectacular failures witness, by contrast, the fundamental goal of Catholicism—the embodiment of the Gospel in all phases of human life.

Whenever Catholic Christianity combined the prophetic missionary spirit of Boniface, the reforming instincts of the Tradition in Pope Gregory, and the constant criticism of the present of an Adso, then the Gospel manifested itself. Church could proclaim support and consolation for the troubled and offer confronting transformation for the sinful and oppressed. When the three moments of Catholicism lost their ability to speak to one another, the dominance of Tradition, prophecy, or apocalyptic visions regularly sent the contemporary culture marching against imaginary enemies or into secluded complacency. That these latter possibilities did not dominate the Catholic Tradition will be seen in the ongoing vigor of the intellectual, spiritual, and political traditions of the High Middle Ages.

NOTES

1. Jean Leclerq, *The Love of Learning and the Desire for God,* trans. Catherine Misrahi (New York: Mentor, 1962).
2. *The Letters of St. Boniface,* trans. Ephraim Emerton (New York: Norton, 1976), 79.
3. Theodore's Penitential, in *Councils and Ecclesiastical Documents Relating to Great Britain and Ireland,* ed. Arthur W. Haddan and William Stubbs (Oxford: At the Clarendon Press, 1964), 3:173–190.
4. Bernard McGinn, *Visions of the End: Apocalyptic Traditions in the Middle Ages* (New York: Columbia University Press, 1979), 62–81.
5. Ibid., 89.

FURTHER RELATED MATERIAL

On monastic theology, one of the finest introductions is Jean Leclerq, *The Love of Learning and the Desire for God,* trans. Catherine Misrahi (New York: Mentor, 1962). R. W. Southern's *Western Society and the Church in the Middle Ages* (Baltimore: Pelican, 1972) emphasizes the social, political, and economic dimensions of the period. Francis Oakley's *The Medieval Experience: Foundations of Western Cultural Singularity* (New York: Charles Scribner's Sons, 1974) stresses the relation of European life to especially non-Western medieval cultures. Bernard McGinn, *Visions of the End: Apocalyptic Traditions in the Middle Ages* (New York: Columbia University Press, 1979) recovers a too frequently neglected aspect of medieval life.

6

THE CULTURE AND CRITICISM OF CHRISTENDOM (1073–1453)

> Born to us, He gave Himself as neighbor;
> At table, He gave Himself as food;
> By dying, He gave Himself as ransom;
> As King, He gives Himself as crown.
> O Saving Victim!
> You open the gate of heaven.
> Hostile wars press us.
> Grant us strength; bring us help.
> > Thomas Aquinas (about 1225–74), from
> > "Verbum Supernum Prodiens."

A period drama in the history of Catholic Christendom occurred at Canossa in the Apennine mountains during January 1077. There Henry IV, emperor of Germany (1056–1106), clothed in the hair shirt of a penitent, knelt shoeless at the gate of a castle, pleading with Pope Gregory VII (1073–85) for release from the ban of excommunication. After three days of prayer and penance Henry was absolved by Gregory and admitted to the Sacrament of the Eucharist. The struggle between empire and Church was decided in favor of ecclesiastical control. Or was it?

The complicated civil machinations which preceded and succeeded this supposed snowy scene actually left Henry with an empire he might otherwise have lost. For in March of that same year, German princes, unhappy that Henry had been released from excommunication, elected a brother-in-law as king.

These sliding loyalties originated in Gregory's attempts to reform the Catholic Church. For the Middle Ages (previously considered a halfway house between Roman antiquity and its humanistic revival in the Italian Renaissance) was a period of struggling reform movements. The successful ones regularly made use of legal and institutional aids to press their claims, electing to high office those who could call the Church to its originating evangelical values.

Medieval Christendom was an uneven ballet among the institutions of empire, priesthood, and academy (*imperium, sacerdotium,* and *studium*). When they moved as partners, there was cultural uniformity, graceful steps which won admiration and participation from all alike. Even while they bickered, limping and staggering, the dancers refused to choose other participants, counting upon their genuinely singular culture to sustain the meaning of their ungainly slips of intelligence, conscience, and power.

During the period when rising technological advantages, burgeoning agricultural plenty, and architectural or sculptural creativity expanded the medieval world, challenges to its cultural unity emerged both without and within. In 1453, the city of Constantinople fell into the hands of the Moslems and the Byzantine Empire died. In the early sixteenth century, Martin Luther's (1483–1546) call for reform of the Church may have echoed earlier voices; but his refusal to allow civil sovereignty over evangelical piety ended the unity of religion and society. Christendom was dead.

The development of Catholic Christianity during these four hundred years is a fascinating story. Uniformity to the culture of Rome predominated as both an ideal and energetic program; yet there remained within the traditional institutions windows to the Church's prophets and visionaries. There was in fact no top-heavy superstructure of boring scholastics and inquisitorial priests, but a genuinely creative tension of architectural forces which vaulted the medieval world into the Christian future.

EMPIRE, CHURCH AND ACADEMY—THE IDEAL OF CULTURAL UNIFORMITY

Attempts to preserve the tradition of the Gospel regularly assumed the form of a promotion and defense of the papacy during the High Middle Ages. The episcopacy of Rome rapidly became the feudal keystone in a hierarchically stratified organization. Just as the differing ministries of priest, reader, cantor, and deacon had collapsed into the single role of priest-celebrant at Eucharistic worship because of scarce liturgical books, so the pope came to be seen as the highest authority within the community, including in his person all the subsidiary ranks of the clergy and laity.

Sacerdotium: The Church as Public Authority

Gregory VII (1073–85) began his reforms of the Church with the Lenten Synods at Rome (1074–75). Noncelibate clerics were forbidden to exercise ecclesiastical roles; laymen and women were encouraged to shun them. Simony, the civil sale and acceptance of religious office, was prohibited. Gregory was unbending: "The Lord did not say, 'I am tradition,' but 'I am truth.'"[1]

Freedom for the Church meant for Gregory separation of ecclesial office from civil entanglements. To free the Church required the extrication of his own power from societal encroachments. A document found among Gregory's letters illustrates this well: "The pope can be judged by no one; the Roman Church has never erred and never will err till the end of time; the pope alone can depose and restore bishops; . . . he alone can revise his own judgments; . . . he can depose emperors; . . . all princes should kiss his feet; . . . a duly ordained pope is undoubtedly made a saint by the merits of St. Peter."[2]

Many of these extravagant claims have their origin in the forged *Donation of Constantine* (see chap. 5); nonetheless they announce an extraordinary proposal for the supreme power of the papal office. Gregory's prohibition of civil nomination for, and investiture in, ecclesiastical office stemmed from his assurance of his own religious dominance. The kingdom of Christ superseded all others.

This claimed and largely achieved primacy of the "Petrine" authority always remains ambiguous in Catholic history. Contemporaries often experienced medieval popes as a voice of religious authority, however much they spoke in the tones of political force. For us, it is easy to lose perspective since we are accustomed to forms of Christianity other than Catholicism. Moreover, attracted to the more humane papal role of recent years, we find the prestige and imperial authority of the medieval popes unpleasant at best, unevangelical at worst.

Gregory could see no way to establish the autonomy of the Gospel without the political legitimacy of episcopal and papal authority. In essence, the vast religious community of medieval Europe practically justified many of his policies. By supporting the establishment of a caste in the celibate clerical bureaucracy, he provided an ecclesial work force divorced in principle from civil control. At its best it could challenge the world's leaders and peoples without indebtedness for food, clothing, or salary; at its worst it merely set up an alternate secular mode, complacent in its own ecclesiastical luxuries.

Imperium: The State as Religious Force— The Crusades and the Inquisitions

The almost incredible mixture of power and Gospel in Gregory, and in the even more famous Innocent III (1198–1216), is obvious to us in both the Crusades against Islam and the Inquisitions against heretics and Jews in the Western Church. The Crusades were nine "holy" wars, stretching from the eleventh through the thirteenth centuries, meant to liberate Palestine and its inhabitants from Islamic overlordship and cultural domination. They were the attempt to impose Western cultural supremacy upon the Eastern Church, Empire, and nonbelieving lands. Their combination of venality and grace, of Gospel and military power, promoted papal authority and served neither Church nor state very well.

If the Crusades were the Church's "external arm" to achieve cultural uniformity, the Inquisitions (lasting from the twelfth through the fifteenth centuries) were its arm to corral the inner cultural and religious dissidents. Any doctrine that did not cohere with the orthodox tradition was proscribed. This included the beliefs of Jews and Moslems as well as heretical Christian doctrines. Confiscation of property, imprisonment, branding, banishment, and even the death penalty were used to ensure compliance. It is said that under Tomás de Torquemada (1420–98), Grand Inquisitor for Isabella of Castile (1451–1504) and Ferdinand of Aragon (1452–1516), some twenty thousand Jews, Moslems, and heterodox Christians were burned by the state.

These sinful horrors of the medieval spirit, however, were not a function of faith, but an excess of devotion to a single cultural ideal. No contemporary Catholic would defend the papal ascendancy, crusading conquests, or inquisitorial strategies against all non-Western, non-Romanized believers. To understand in this case is not to absolve; responsibility for brutality cannot be erased by locating procedures inside historical eventualities. The coercive use of force lodges as a dangerous memory of human suffering which cannot be forgotten except at the price of further inhumanity. Like a chastened individual, the Catholic Tradition must repay the faults of sinners in its past by championing justice for the oppressed in its present.

The High Middle Ages believed that there could be only one civil culture with one religious force, just as a body could contain only a single animating soul. What had been bequeathed by the early Middle Ages as a vibrant prophetic attempt to enliven culture by faith grew into an unwieldly adolescent of uncertain parentage and an adult of fierce, unholy demeanor. It was a religious internationalism which could embody itself solely through a uniform religious and civil practice.

Studium: The Academy as Theologian

An intellectual development made possible by Christendom remains a vital force in contemporary Catholic life—academic theology and the university. The theoretic and systematic achievements of medieval canon lawyers and theologians provided an extraordinary intellectual support for, as well as criticism of, the public institution. In thinkers such as Thomas Aquinas (about 1225–74), Bonaventure (about 1217–74), Roger Bacon (1212–94), and Raymond Lull (1235–1316), as well as in lesser known men and women, intellectual classics transcended the doctrines of the age.

Conflicting Legal Interpretations

Ivo of Chartres (about 1040–1115) systematized the multiple collections of law that accumulated from the fifth through ninth centuries. Following him, Gratian (+1159), in his *Concordance of Discordant Canons,* provided a collection which until 1917 was the basis of all Catholic legislation. Gratian's style of reasoning combined a question, texts, and arguments for and against an answer and then reconciliation of disagreements. This scholarly comprehensive moderation established the shape of medieval scholastic thought.

Conflicting Biblical Interpretations

What the lawyers first accomplished appeared rapidly as a theological development. Just as the reflections on the earliest traditions had originated in the biblical images and stories, and doctrines had emerged to maintain the legitimate outlines of belief in a new culture, there was now a need to clarify just how these various understandings could be ordered.

Accurate readings of the biblical texts and consistent commentary were provided through the School of Laon (about 1100), when Anselm, Ralph, and Gilbert the Universal completed *The Ordinary Gloss (Glossa Ordinaria)* as a basic textbook for the monastic and cathedral schools. Stephen Langton (+1228) divided the books of the Bible into chapters and verses, a practice which made reference considerably simpler. His work, with small modification, is still in use.

The Thrust Toward System: Scholasticism

While the basic materials were being solidified, theologians, first in northern France, then in Paris and Chartres, attempted to order the Christian message into a system. In this they were dependent upon philosophic tools made available to them through the intellectual labors of Ibn-Sina (Avicenna, 980–1037), who combined Aristotelian and Platonic theories of knowledge in a religious context, and Ibn-Rushd (Averroes, 1126–98), whose creative commentaries upon the texts of Aristotle earned him the title "The Commentator." Western theologians had before them the examples of Origen (185–254), who used Middle Platonic thought to arrange Christian questions into a whole, and the descriptions of Pseudo-Dionysius (about 500), whose cosmological mysticism painted a symbolic picture of the universe.

The "masters of the sacred page" and their expositions of Scripture were thus succeeded by the theologians. Hugh of St. Victor in Paris (1096–1141) set for himself the goal of rewriting Augustine's whole project for the Middle Ages. Anselm of Canterbury (about 1033–1109), however, is the acknowledged father of Scholasticism. His philosophical argument for the existence of God still teases thinkers. God is that than which nothing greater can be thought. But to exist in reality is greater than to exist merely in thought. Therefore God must exist.

Such ingenuity encompassed the entire range of theological issues but especially those of salvation itself. Why *did* God become a human being? At the same time that he was extricating the Church from the power of his king, Anselm did not think it blasphemous to ask questions of God's Word and to construct intelligent answers.

He clearly believed that since God gave us both reason and faith, the two could not ultimately be in conflict. Life was a matter of "faith seeking understanding" (*fides quaerens intellectum*), a definition of theology as a discipline which has never been superseded.

The School of Chartres turned to questions of physics, culture, and religion. Could the literal meaning of the Bible be coherent with the physics available in Plato's accounts of the origins of the world (an earlier version of the creationism-evolution debates)? If natural causes will explain an event, must we appeal to God as cause?

Conservative Reaction

Such questions frightened some believers. For rather than supporting some extrinsically derived thought-system, these theologians marched around the edges of the empire of faith. Not all Christians wished to go further than the well-traveled pilgrimage routes; they preferred to have their ordinary sacramental companions and local authoritative assurances. This problem may be seen in a preeminent controversy between Peter Abelard (1079–1142) and Bernard of Clairvaux (1090–1153). Bernard speaks first: "[Abelard] points his mouth to the heavens and looks into the depths of God; looking back, he returns ineffable words not permitted a man to speak. Moreover, he has provided a reason for everything, even those things which are above reason, even against reason and against faith. . . . What could be more against faith than to refuse to believe whatever one is not able to attain by reason?"[3]

Monastic theology emphasized the experience of faith, not its rational interpretation. Its primary daily task was "divine reading" (*lectio divina*), which permitted assimilation of the biblical and theological tradition in a personal and communitarian fashion. Bernard himself thought the object of *theologia* (the logic of God) was to know Christ crucified; one could not achieve that knowledge without prayer and a considerable degree of humility. As a result of this theological process, we learn to love ourselves as God loves us. Rupert of Deutz (about 1075–1129) confirmed this in a sharp formulation: "Whatever can be thought up apart from sacred scripture or fabricated out of argumentation is unreasonable; and therefore pertains in no way to the praise or the acknowledgement of the omnipotence of God."[4]

Abelard, a brilliant and passionate teacher, developed a theologi-

67

cal method which occasioned this abuse. Indeed he is the first thinker to use the word "theology" in its contemporary sense as rational thought about the Divine; before him, it had included prayer, sacraments, hymns—all religious expressions. In his *Sic et Non* (1121–22) he set an intellectual standard against which all later thinkers were required to measure themselves. Setting standards does not make a thinker popular—particularly when that thinker is as embroiled in moral and religious controversy as Abelard was. (We need only recall the story of his love for Heloise [1101–64] to be reminded of such arguments.)

The text of *Sic et Non* takes 158 questions left unanswered by the authorities and marshals the opposing viewpoints under them. In his introduction Abelard offers general rules for deciding which authority to follow, paralleling those of the canonists. The major conflict with opponents like Bernard is that he did not choose to resolve serious questions in a pious way. He let them simply stand. The authorities who conflicted were the traditional fathers of the community. Thus contemporary minds were setting themselves up as judges over their traditional past. For Bernard this was utter arrogance.

Aristotle's Assistance

Human pride in this case was leavened by the successive entries of the philosopher Aristotle into Western European thought. For before the twelfth century, there was only a meager amount of the thinker's works available: the *Categories* and *On Interpretation*, generally called the Grammar or Old Logic. But between 1140–60 Aristotle's *Sophistical Refutations* and the *Prior* and *Posterior Analytics* were translated, known as the New Logic or Dialectics. The majority of Aristotle's works, all those of strictly philosophical rather than simply logical interest (physics, psychology, metaphysics, ethics, and politics) were not translated until 1240–50.

Aristotle's analyses created a vast sea-change in religious circles. Thinking Christianity through Aristotle resulted in a more terrestrial, empirical, and scientific approach to God and God's dealings with human beings. What Bernard thought of Abelard can be encapsulated under those three adjectives: his theology was not sufficiently heaven-directed, spiritual, or homiletic. It could not be Christian. It was dependent on the first and second entries of Aristotle.

The inclusion of Aristotle's thought as a way of seeing the world thoroughly and scientifically with religious faith took some time. It was only as Catholics began to see religious benefits from it that such endeavors became more than merely suspect.

Teacher and Textbook

Peter the Lombard (+1159) helped in that process. For what Abelard left unanswered, Peter resolved. As a result his *Liber Sententiarum* (*Book of Sentences,* i.e., opinions) became a standard lecturing textbook for theologians well into the seventeenth century. He ordered all Christian questions around four basic topics: God; creation and the history of the world before Christ; the incarnation and redemption in Christ; and the sacraments and eschatology. Under those headings, he posed the various questions which were current, outlined the authorities for and against, and made a judgment about which were valid.

Like all textbooks, it had a common-sense approach; and common sense, while resolving many difficulties in our ordinary religious world, regularly leaves some assumptions unexamined. Yet its lucid organization, clear exposition, and ready answers made it a landmark in scholastic method. The question itself had become a tool of theological research; its resolutions depended upon the understanding of Christ and the cultural, intellectual embodiment attained by the thinker.

Thomas Aquinas

Although there were other scholastics during the "Golden Age" of the thirteenth century, none is the peer of Thomas Aquinas (about 1225–74). In the battle of authorities, Aquinas commented: "If the master determines the question by an appeal to authorities only, the student will be convinced that the thing is so; but he will have acquired no knowledge or understanding and will go away with an empty head."[5] Aquinas was on the side of "faith seeking understanding" through whatever scientific tools were available.

Aquinas noticed first that the objects of religion (God and the world in God) have a certain oddity about them. They are present, but not available to us in exactly the same way as other physical things. To provide a language for understanding them, we need a *meta*-physical language, a body of terms and relations which will help us distinguish the location of religion among other realities in our world. He found that theoretic set of terms in Aristotle's metaphysics. To understand the other pole of the gracious act of God's love, humanity, Aquinas reinterpreted Aristotle's rational psychological texts so that he could unravel the knowing process itself.

Religion was different from philosophy. Where the principles of reality presented themselves to philosophy after sometimes difficult thought, in Christianity the principles (namely God as Triune) revealed themselves. Theology for Aquinas was first of all God's own knowledge of himself. God alone knows who he truly is; for creatures to become aware of him, God must disclose himself to us. All knowledge about God, whether faith, theology (as the understanding of faith), or final union with God, is dependent upon the one Teacher. Theology is thus not geometry, whose principles can be discovered by reason itself.

If the science of faith becomes a habit or second nature to us, then we can depend upon our own intellect for some reasonable explication of religious faith. But even thought itself is affected by pride, so we require the assistance of the Holy Spirit to achieve true wisdom. Theology is not merely a speculative discipline. It includes both thought and action. Theology is directed toward the good and the beautiful as well as to what is true.

With this understanding of reason and faith, Aquinas wrote his *Summaries (Summae)* of theology. Now summary could be a misleading term, since what Aquinas prepared was a reasoned, systematic expression of the understanding that a scientifically trained individual might reach. Where Hugh of St. Victor might use symbolic language or Peter Abelard might simply set up oppositions to tease the mind, Aquinas marshaled all his forces. He knew the intellectual terrain, had clarified and distinguished the different types of personnel and material available, and pondered the tactics which would accomplish the goal. His *Summa* is rather like a strategic map of the Christian religious world. Those who wish to find their way a little can follow his lead; those who will complete the campaign must duplicate in their own experience of faith the relationships envisioned. It is a masterful achievement. All things come from the Triune God as origin and all things return to that God. The image of

God which was lost through sin after creation is regained as a likeness to God, a share in his divinity through the one Way: Christ.

A mind critical of the intellectual aspects of life might be tempted to think that nothing so scientific could really remain religious. Yet Aquinas not only thought, he also prayed, preached, and composed religious poetry. He was so profoundly moved by what was at stake in the Christian experience that he joined the new order of mendicant (begging) preachers formed by Dominic (1170–1221). He did not hesitate to reject his family's wealth and position in order to obey the Christian Gospel's command for simplicity and poverty. But at the same time he dared to employ in his own faith the pagan, worldly thinker Aristotle.

Universities as Religious Criticism

This was a world of university theology, an academic lever of criticism raised in support of, but sometimes against, the political and ecclesiastical institutions. The survivors of the old cathedral and monastic schools had banded together, drawn up constitutions, and obtained important exemptions which guaranteed the student body personal safety, administrative autonomy, exemption from taxation, and the right to confer teaching licenses.

From the late twelfth century, Paris developed a *universitas magistrorum* (university of teachers) which was given statutes by Pope Innocent III in 1215, primarily centered upon the faculties of theology, law, medicine, and the liberal arts. Chartered schools appeared all over Europe: Bologna (twelfth century), Toulouse (1229), Rome (1244), Naples (1224), and Salamanca (1243). But Paris remained the most famous for philosophy and theology; it numbered among its teachers Thomas Aquinas, Bonaventure, William of Auxerre (+1231), and a Latin Averroist named Siger of Brabant (about 1240–84). By the year 1300 there was an estimated student population in Paris of thirty thousand.

With scholastic thought, Christians had come of intellectual age. They had learned to live in the house of religion and understand its structure scientifically without trying to pretend that the mystery of God's grace in Christ would ever be exhaustively explained. With Scholasticism Catholics no longer felt compelled to choose between faith and reason. They discovered a way to distinguish these two central dimensions of their lives in order to reunite them in a single edifice of wisdom founded upon the Gospel.

Places of Prayer

Diversity collaborated to produce unity in high Gothic art as well. In 1231, at the same time that Alexander of Hales (+1245), a Franciscan scholastic of considerable merit, began the earliest *Summa,* the architect Pierre de Montreuil (about 1200–1266) conceived the new nave of the Church of St. Denis outside Paris. Just as Aquinas's *Summa Theologiae* hoped to include within its interpretation all elements of Christian experience and understanding, distinguishing, balancing, supporting, and eliminating the fruitless consequence, so the Gothic cathedral aimed at a totality. Chartres, dedicated in 1260, enshrined on its facade a sculptural program encompassing all time and space emanating from the dawn of the triumphal Christ. The plastic light from the brilliant windows wrapped the believer in an entire range of colors and shapes, tracing all the major themes of the Bible.

In the Middle Ages spirit met flesh in a most uncompromisingly ordinary fashion. For the shrines of medieval Christendom with their glowing jewels for windows and biblical inspiration housed a motley populace who arrived on pilgrimage to heaven. Perhaps nowhere for the English-speaking reader is this more evident than in Geoffrey Chaucer's (about 1343–1400) *Canterbury Tales.* For what Chartres was to French Christians and Campostella to Spaniards, Canterbury's shrine to the royal martyr Thomas à Becket (about 1118–70) was to English pilgrims.

Though unfinished, Chaucer's *Canterbury Tales* reflects that sophisticated knowledge of human beings which can combine compassion for weakness with irony over ideals unfulfilled, intelligent criticism of the goals of society with an intricate understanding of their interpersonal complexities. His pilgrims are monks who love hunting, prioresses who combine prayer and aristocratic manners, dignified merchants and not-so-stately or aristocratic cooks, millers, pardoners, and estate managers. The whole tapestry of medieval life is woven into his poetry; the figures are sprightly, the background filled with thousands of flowers.

But the keystone of medieval society was religion. So Chaucer, quite capable of attacking ecclesiastical abuse, described an ideal parish priest as rich in thought and work, patient, diligent, and devout. Instead of receiving tithes, he gave from his own substance to his parishioners. He did not think twice about criticizing the rich or powerful. As Chaucer says:

> But Christes lore, and his apostles twelve,
> He taught, and first he followed it himself.[6]

Chaucer knew both ideal and real; his art reflected reality, challenged it, and awakened the world to its own best possibilities.

The experience of turning the Tradition of Catholicism into a solid building to house the diversity of Christian prayer founded upon the Gospel was the project of medieval Christendom. The papacy, scholasticism, and civil government collaborated (in their best moments) to provide a unified Tradition of prayer, thought, and action which would incarnate again the event of Christ. Their achievements contained difficulties and limitations exploited later. But the vision and its not inconsiderable accomplishment in classics like Gregory, Aquinas, or Chartres should teach us something very important about the fierce conviction of Catholicism that the Tradition of symbols, sacraments, doctrines, institutional office, and intellectual endeavor can authentically disclose the Gospel of Jesus.

PROPHETS AND VISIONARIES: BEGGARS AND PREACHERS

The counterpoint to the institutional Tradition in the Middle Ages is to be found in the rise of the mendicant or begging orders like the Franciscans and Dominicans. Men like Francis of Assisi (about 1132–1226), his more intellectual followers like Bonaventure (1221–74) or Dominic (1170–1221), and Robert of Molesme (about 1027–1111), who founded a strictly contemplative community, spoke for the edges of human experience, whether it was through their dedication to poverty, prayerful silence, or preaching to the remaining unchurched barbarians.

These communities of reform, though they seem marginal to us now, were each called to embody the radical demands of the Gospel. Indeed it is the very marginality of monastic life that Thomas Merton

(1915–68), a Trappist monk in Kentucky, saw as important to society. He spoke of the monk as one who stands on the edge between words and silence, between sociocultural construction and the evangelical values which must inform them, between action and contemplation. Such men and women are never escape artists, or bystanders; rather they always alert the Catholic Church to its common call to holiness.

Such prophets were paralleled by men and women like Joachim of Flora (1135–1202) or the author of *Piers Plowman* (about mid-fourteenth century) who through a steady application of the ideals of Scripture to their contemporary life startled the late medieval world from complacency. Seized by the pain of the shifting cultures of their day, they prompted traditions of thought which were revolutionary and radical.

THE DECLINE OF CHRISTENDOM AND VISIONS OF UNITY

The Great Western Schism (1378–1417) occurred in the Catholic Church when French cardinals, having returned to Rome after residence in Avignon for many years (1309–77), elected an opposition candidate for pope (Clement VII, 1378–94). National feelings controlled the conflicts for almost forty years, with first one, then another pope claiming ascendancy. Some Christians knew a world in which there were always two, even three, popes. Some dioceses had two or three claimants for office. The luxury of the Avignonese papacy ceded to a dreadful collapse of Christian unity. There was a growing split between national consciousness and religious loyalty. Allegiance by baptism to the local Church was not necessarily support of the local or imperial prince; and political fealty might require opposition to the religious pretensions of a papal lord.

If, however, much of this controversy seems too refined in its enthusiasm to catch our interest, too complex in its loyalties to help us understand the Gospel, Dante's *Divine Comedy* does not. Dante Alighieri (1265–1321) described Christian life as a pilgrimage through three worlds: Hell, Purgatory, and Paradise. He was prophetic in his ability to incarnate Christian experience in the poetic language of his own people; he was traditional not only in founding a tradition of poetry and language, but in embodying the philosophical tradition of Scholasticism; he was apocalyptic in that he knew that only criticism of the present could afford glimpses of the future world that God offers.

Decline and vision marked the end of Christendom. The unanswered questions of the High Middle Ages, the relationship of civil and religious power, and, even more fundamentally, the nature of Christian salvation seethed at the surface, boiling over into the passions of the Reformation.

By the end of the Middle Ages these issues polarized the situation. Either faith or reason, religion or Scholasticism; either our works or God's grace, merit or redemption; either the literal meaning of Scripture or allegory, fact or fiction; either popular sovereignty in aid of the rising national states or the authority of an international prince, whether emperor or pope.

Decade by decade, the traditional bridges which had integrated each pole into a common vision of society, Church, and God's love were disintegrating. It was as though a river which Christians knew over generations had changed its shoreline, and only gradually did everyone realize that the old bridges would no longer transport people where they wanted to go. The classic roads remained; but the language of a *Summa,* a Gothic cathedral, even a *Divine Comedy* seemed antiquated, rather unsafe, misplaced since the banks of the river had changed. Where was the bridge-building expert in this crisis of Christendom?

NOTES

1. Quoted in Francis Oakley, *The Medieval Experience: Foundations of Western Cultural Singularity* (New York: Charles Scribner's Sons, 1974), 34.

2. Gregorii VII Registrum, *Monumenta Germaniae Historiae,* Epistolae Selectae, ii, ed. E. Casper, pp. 201–8 as cited in R. W. Southern, *Western Society and the Church in the Middle Ages* (Baltimore: Penguin Books, 1972), 102.

3. Letter to Pope Innocent, No. CXC in *Works of St. Bernard,* ed. Jean LeClerq and H. Rochais (Rome: Cistercian Editions, 1977), 8:17–18.

4. *De Omnipotentia Dei,* chap. 27; *Patrologia Latina,* ed. J. P. Migne (Paris, 1854), CLXX, col. 478.

5. *Quodlibetal Questions* IV, question IX, article XVIII.

6. General Prologue, Geoffrey Chaucer, *Canterbury Tales*, 2:528–530 in *The Works of Geoffrey Chaucer*, ed. F. N. Robinson (Boston: Houghton Mifflin, 1961), 22.

FURTHER RELATED MATERIAL

Much has been written on medieval universities, theologians, and politics. A delightful introduction to university theology is Helen Waddell's *The Wandering Scholars* (Garden City, N.Y.: Doubleday & Co., 1961). An important series of essays, though difficult, is M-D. Chenu, *Man, Nature and Society in the Twelfth Century* (Chicago: University of Chicago Press, 1967). David Knowles's *The Evolution of Medieval Thought* (New York: Vintage, 1962) almost bristles too much with names, places, and ideas while Étienne Gilson's classic *History of Christian Philosophy in the Middle Ages* (New York: Random House, 1955) can occupy the very serious student of the period. James Weisheipl's biography of Thomas Aquinas, *Friar Thomas d'Aquino: His Life, Thought and Works* (New York: Harper & Row, 1974), is excellent along with the classic M-D. Chenu, *Toward Understanding St. Thomas* (Chicago: Regnery, 1964).

THE CRIES FOR
REFORM AND THE RISE OF
RELIGIOUS SUBJECTIVITY (1400–1622)

> Why are the times so dark,
> Such that no man knows another?
> For governments meander, as we see,
> From bad to worse without recourse.
> Times past seemed so much better.
> Who reigns? Sadness and annoyance!
> Neither Justice nor Law walk the streets.
> I do not know where I stand.
> > Eustache Deschamps (1346–1406)[1]

After a lengthy debate with his conscience, Martin Luther (1483–1546) knew where he stood—captive to the Word of God. "I cannot and I will not recant anything, for to go against conscience is neither right nor safe. God help me. Amen. Here I stand. I cannot do otherwise." Thus sharply is Luther's speech reported before the Catholic Emperor Charles V (1500–1588) and his electors at the Diet of Worms (1521). The wandering Church and society of the fourteenth century, tortured by wars, political hatred, and lack of confidence in its own confessions, had coalesced through a new energy. But there was an enormous ransom paid for this new direction—nothing less than the division of Western Christendom.

No single origin can be named. The events issued from knotted ropes of sincere religious motivations, civil opportunism, and cultural determining factors far beyond the participants themselves. The quiet reasoners and prudent administrators who could conduct the choruses of prophets or visionaries against the solo voices of Tradition were not heard. At the conclusion of the sixteenth century the oratorio of medieval Christendom had grown discordant.

Required by custom to fight their battles as a secular state, popes, cardinals, and bishops financed their political causes through the religious "goods" available to them. Bishoprics and indulgences were sold to the highest bidder. Simultaneously, a rising nationalism among the emergent states of Europe harnessed religious reform movements and drove them to their own ends. A Church less closely connected with Rome meant a Church more subject to local civil control. Nor was it easy for rulers in need of money for consolidation of power to ignore the extensive economic holdings of the Church, especially those of the monasteries.

Yet the religious impulse for reform was dominant, if not always heeded. Jan Hus (about 1372–1415) remarked: "I desired in preaching to obey only God rather than the pope or the archbishop and the rest of the satraps opposing the word of Christ."[2] Hus's combination of anger and religious zeal won him a heretic's death at the Council of Constance (1414–17).

The passions produced by the visible corruption of the traditional instruments of spirituality cannot be easily measured. The ideals announced by the sacramental spectacles of the Church were separated from ordinary Christian lives. The visionary Joachim of Flora (about 1132–1202) believed that in the age to come, the primary participants would be monks and friars—not married men and women. Religion had become something to watch from afar—rather than a prayerful event common to baptized participants. Its application to the lives of believers focused upon the historical past of Jesus' life, rather than upon contemporary ecclesial achievement.

Yet by the end of the sixteenth century, Christianity had finally reformed itself into two competing branches: Protestant and Catholic. Only with the discussions for reunion in our own time (the ecumenical movement) have the two arms of Western Christianity viewed the turmoil of these years with less distorted vision. Though faithful to their own traditions, Catholic and Protestant historians of this century, humbled by the knowledge that angry arguments have only contributed to a belittled Christian Gospel, now read and write with historical rigor and ecumenical compassion.

The modern meaning of Catholicism cannot be understood without reference to the questions, concerns, and passions of Protestant reformers. The reformulation of the Catholic Church after the division of Christendom, although coherent and consistent with its previous Tradition, has been affected by the sometimes peaceful, sometimes violent conversations with its familial relations.

THE NEED FOR REFORM

Reform is a critical principle in human affairs—a negative reaction to what speciously passes for truth, justice, or love. The popular fervor of the late Middle Ages was a passion for the sensible, whether sacred or profane. Some relatively brief, largely benign examples may show what we mean.[3]

Peter of Luxembourg (1369–87) cultivated hardship. He wanted to preach the Gospel; his parents opposed it, so he became an eccentric ascetic instead. As William James was to say of a later figure: "In this poor man, we have morbid melancholy and fear, and the sacrifices made are to purge out sin and to buy safety."[4] Unwashed, sickly, covered with lice, Peter copied his sins in small notebooks. At his death, an entire chest of small scraps (kept for his confessor) was found. A bishop at fifteen, then a cardinal, Peter's case for canonization was assured at death—since all the lords of France testified to his sanctity *and* to his devotion to the French pope in the Great Western Schism. His holiness was witnessed concretely—by his healing of tournament wounds, the resurrection of a steward struck by a thunderbolt, and the salvation of the Duchess of Bourbon from two weeks of labor pains.

This example of the "underwitted saint" (as James might have called him) should be paralleled by the chronicler's description of the Great Entrance of Louis XI (1423–83) at the time of his coronation (1461). The historian speaks of "three very handsome girls, representing quite naked sirens, and one saw their beautiful, turgid, separate, round, and hard breasts, which was a very pleasant sight, and they recited little motets and bergerettes." Such nude spectacles were not uncommon during the entire century.

The late Middle Ages needed visible evidence of the meaningfulness of life. Sacramental piety focused on a growing devotion to the presence of Christ in the Eucharistic Supper. Although the Feast of Corpus Christi (the Body of Christ) had been ordered part of the universal religious calendar by 1264, it was the fourteenth century that tells us about the Sacrament reserved in the hand of a silver statue of the Virgin Mary, placed above the high altar.[5]

Nor was this grasping for the concrete Divine limited to the visual. Medieval preaching required the startling sensible example to ensure effectiveness. The Archpriest of Talavera, Alfonso Martinez de Toledo (1398–1466/70) details human avarice and lust through copious earthy stories.

> I knew one such whose house was always full of this nonsense, an old hag of seventy. I saw her hanged from the balcony of a man she had murdered by applying poison to his armpits; and they also hanged her by the neck at the door of a matron that she had killed, and burned her later for a witch at Caned, outside the city; nor was she saved by the great favor she enjoyed with many gentlemen.[6]

There was a constant need to reify the religious impulse.

Perhaps it is this somewhat fleshy sedimentation that accounts for the uncompromising venality of so many Renaissance and early Reformation popes. One cannot but be scandalized by the paradox of religious sentiment, artistic splendor, and vulgar opportunism. In the nepotism of Innocent VIII (1484–92) for his illegitimate family, the bribed election and open concubinage of Alexander VI (1492–1503), Julius II's (1503–13) military programs, and the cultured laxism of Leo X (1513–21), we see the squandering of centralized papal power on debauchery and personal ambition. Their lethargy, avarice, and politically self-serving prudence, though sometimes exaggerated by Reformers' polemics, did not rise above the same vices in their secular contemporaries. Hilaire Belloc (1870–1953), that most Catholic historian, remarks that because they had not returned to their evangelical origins, the external organizers of the Church had failed to "capture the spiritual discontent and to satisfy the spiritual hunger of which these errors were the manifestation."[7]

THE CENTERS OF OPPOSITION

Three movements contributed to the critique of religious arrogance and corruption: *conciliarism* in ecclesiastical polity; *nominalism and Ockhamism* in academic thought; and *humanist scholarship* in religious piety. Each was a profoundly dialectical move within Catholic experience; each suspected the reigning common sense of having tipped the incarnational balance of the Gospel on the side of secularizing leaden weights. Although we can only briefly indicate the issues raised by each complex development, we must do so to set the stage for Luther's dramatic entrance.

Conciliarism—The Pride of the Papacy

Conciliarism wished to vest the ultimate authority of ecclesial life in a general council. Its theory began simultaneously with the rise of papal power but grew in cogency during the Great Western Schism. Because the Council of Constance (1414–17) was largely successful in its attempts to end the Schism, the fathers decreed reforms which entailed periodic general councils to settle ecclesiastical affairs. But these largely died in the later administration of reforms which were to be settled through rather weak concordats between the papacy and national groupings. In 1460 Pius II (1458–64) prohibited all appeals from papal decisions to general councils.

Ockhamism—The Arrogance of the Academy

If conciliarism was a plea for decentralization of authoritarian rule in the Church and release from supranational taxation, nominalism was a critique directed at the arrogance of reason in matters of faith. William of Ockham (1285–1347), though perhaps not strictly a nominalist himself, emphasized that our knowledge can be only of the singulars in the empirical world. Thus without divine revelation we would never know any intrinsic connection between the world and God. Ockham's anger was directed against all those inter-mediaries who pretended to assume responsibility and knowledge of the divine plan. His philosophical, or perhaps better said, logical, positions were meant to preserve the sovereignty of God's free action from any limitations imposed upon that absolute power by over-weening Scholasticism and politics.

Humanism—The Hubris of Religious Abstraction

Medieval piety stressed the accumulation of ascetical merit and passive participation in sacramental spectacles. It was criticized by those who emphasized mystical religious experience, by those who sought a "modern piety" (*devotio moderna*), and by historical and biblical scholars.

Luther's personal anxiety for salvation appeared within a Tradition of mystics who, like Meister Eckhart (1260–1327), presented religion in a deeply affecting German. For Eckhart, to live as God does meant to be utterly selfless, without possession, separated from the idols we have of self, world, and God. Along with John Tauler (about 1300–1361), Henry Suso, (about 1295–1366), and others, Eckhart preached a return to interiorized religious development.

This homiletic invitation was encouraged further by a movement of lay-centered piety founded by Gerhard Groote (1340–84). The Brethren of the Common Life, living a quasi-monastic communitarian life in Deventer, The Netherlands, were never meant to be clerics. They were contemplatives who continued their ordinary vocations, only later establishing schools where a general education was offered without fee. Numerous reformers such as Pope Hadrian VI (1522–23), Gabriel Biel (about 1420–95), and Nicholas of Cusa (1401–64) came through their doors. But perhaps the brother with the longest popular history was Thomas à Kempis (1380–1471), whose small work, *The Imitation of Christ,* has taught Catholics for centuries how to seek perfection by putting on Christ as a model of life.

It is from these religious circles that there emerged humanist scholarship such as that of the eternally intriguing thinker Desiderius Erasmus (about 1469–1536). A truly international scholar, he taught in Paris, Louvain, and finally housed himself in Basel with the printer Froben (about 1460–1527). Through this printing house, Erasmus provided the Western Church with its first critical edition of the Greek New Testament (1516). Prior to this the Church had been dependent upon Jerome's (about 342–420) Latin edition (the *Vulgate*). Only by returning to the authentic sources of Catholic Christianity could the Church reform itself properly. When at Thomas More's (1478–1535) home in England, Erasmus wrote *In Praise of Folly* (1509), a sharp diatribe against civil and ecclesiastical abuse. But despite his constant arguments against pious confusions, religious lukewarmness, and institutional stupidity, Erasmus could not envision a separated Church as a Gospel value.

The criticisms of the Church from within its ranks should have provided the ferment for a revitalization of the community. Although there were many figures like John Gerson (1363–1429), doctor of theology, chancellor of the University of Paris and untiring champion of reform, others possessed a fundamental failure of vision. The divisive reform of the early sixteenth century was an inability to reenvision the world after all the criticisms (conciliarism, nominalism, humanism). No one seemed capable of seeing how the prophetic, visionary, *and* traditional moments of Catholic life could be encompassed within a single polity.

No one really wanted the somewhat elderly gentleman whose irascibility, incorrigible behavior, and inflexible character made him seem incapable of recovering his religious youth. Many no longer believed that he could remain a member of the family as it met new crises, faced new problems, and learned new skills. With the Catholic partners in earlier fertile dialogue now insulated from one another by anger and political protectionism, there was scant opportunity to forgive the sins of the old Church or welcome anything but the rival siblings of the new.

PROPHETIC QUESTIONS

It is appropriate, but inadequate, to describe the major Protestant Reformers briefly. Since this is the story of Catholicism, we can only barely indicate some of the questions and concerns raised by major figures and leave further explication to others. The danger is oversimplification; but if the questions raised are taken as the fruit of the Reformers' lifelong quests for religious understanding, the desire for civil and ecclesiastical justice, and hope for gradual change dashed, then we will have been mildly successful.

We may take as representative three men: Martin Luther (1483–1546), Ulrich Zwingli (1484–1531), and John Calvin (1509–64). If the first was a religious prophet and the second a rather radical political visionary, the third was a consolidator of the new Tradition.

Martin Luther

Luther's questions emerged from his own acute struggle with the absolute graciousness of God's love over all attempts by human beings to justify themselves. Can anyone merit or earn God's grace? This believer in the monastic experiential Tradition responded with a thundering "No." In his three reforming treatises of 1520 (*To the*

German Princes; On the Babylonian Captivity of the Church; Concerning the Freedom of Christians), he appealed to civil authorities to take ecclesiastical reform into their own hands: to forbid taxation by Rome, to abolish the celibacy of the clergy, to disallow religious orders' exemption from local rule, and to reformulate the internal religious policies of worship and morality. All religious answers must conform to the norm of the gracious Word of God as found in the Scriptures.

Ulrich Zwingli and Thomas Münzer

Ulrich Zwingli carried the reformed position one step further: "There is no vehicle necessary for the Spirit."[8] All concrete manifestations of Christendom (whether sacramental, institutional, ascetical, or artistic) were divorced from the inner life of the believer. If Catholic critics were concerned that Luther's position would favor a personalized private conscience, they knew that Zwingli's preaching was even more dangerous. Pictures were removed, images smashed, Eucharist was limited to a few times a year. But the Zwinglian question still haunted European Reformers: Which mediations of God's grace are authentically Christian? Are *any* to be preferred to the internal witness of the Spirit?

Zwingli's religious radicality was paralleled by his political involvement. He sought independence from papal intervention for Swiss cantons. He is rivaled only by Thomas Münzer (about 1490–1525) in his engagement for civil freedoms. "Don't put up any shallow pretense that God's might will do it without your laying on with the sword."[9] Münzer's armed insurrection to establish a Christian millennial age was stopped when Luther invited the German lords to crush the Peasants' Revolt (1525). The unthinking brutality of powerful institutions begot the power of thoughtless violence.

John Calvin

But Zwingli's and Münzer's underlying problem with the old Christian polity remained. How do we establish a Christian civil government? Is there a public form to Christian love? John Calvin attempted to reconstitute Christendom as a fragment of itself in Geneva. He hoped to revive Christian life by imitating the ancient Church. His *Institutes of the Christian Religion* grew from a small catechism into a grand Protestant *summa* of theological synthesis in which the sovereignty of God's wisdom and love elects some to share in divine glory. Calvin's combination of a helpful ecclesiastical order, sharply defined scriptural exegesis, notionally distinct doctrinal positions, and deep religious conviction made his interpretation of the Reform necessary in a situation in growing need of organization. Calvin carefully, though sometimes ruthlessly, institutionalized the reforming Tradition.

THE REFORM OF TRADITIONAL CATHOLICISM—
THE COUNCIL OF TRENT

If the prophets and apocalyptic visionaries had largely separated themselves from the ecclesiastical authority, what did the institution have to say for itself? Traditional Catholicism, prodded by the growing external forces of reform, and pulled, sometimes quite reluctantly, by its own ardently loyal leaders, haltingly reconstituted itself, a fragment of a whole and reestablished an alternate Christendom to Lutheran, Calvinist, and Zwinglian Churches.

As the most clearminded Catholic reformers knew, only a general council could revive the religious dry bones. Yet just as Luther could not ignore the German princes in his quest for religious freedom, so Catholic need for religious reform was not the sole consideration in the calls for and against a general council. Too many kings and petty princes wanted not so much to reform Rome as to embarrass their secular rivals, the Renaissance popes and their changing allies. The popes wanted reform, but only if their civil independence was maintained. Fortunately the council overcame political opposition, and Pope Paul III (1534–49) called for an extraordinary gathering of theologians, bishops, cardinals, and national representatives in December 1545. The Council begun at Trent was to survive eighteen years of intensive, if necessarily sporadic, labor, three major sessions, and five popes.

Its final results were mixed in character, but were without doubt in the reforming Tradition. On the negative side, the Council of Trent did not achieve—in fact, it did not even attempt what had by then probably become an impossibility—reunion with the Protestants. As a result of this failure, many of its decrees and canons were so critical of Reformers' positions that they ensured that the break would be irreparable.

But positively, Trent made impressive gains since Catholic reformers carried the day. There were remarkable men, such as Gasparo Contarini (1483–1542), who worked tirelessly for reunion; Jerome Seripando (1492–1563), general of Luther's former religious community and chief representative of Augustinianism at the council, and Reginald Pole (1500–1558), archbishop of Canterbury, who led the council in its earlier sessions. In the last session, Charles Borromeo (1538–84), of considerable acumen in Scripture, doctrine, and religious education, directed the council's carefully worded, lucid statements on the whole range of Catholic disciplinary and doctrinal questions.

The Council formulated a view of justification by faith that asserted God's prior Word of love before, during, and after our human choice to love God; but it did so in the context of a scripturally based and nuanced understanding of human development and change. We are saved by and in Christ. All subtle attempts to vitiate human responsibility or divine love, whether by negating human choice (Luther) or by exalting it to self-salvation (Pelagius), are rejected.

Simultaneously, practical reforms were issued. Where the Protestant reformers focused on raising the religious literacy of the ordinary Christian, Catholic Tradition leveled its primary broadsides at the disciplinary life of its Church leaders. Seminaries for the education of clerics were to be formed in all major dioceses to ensure that future priests and bishops would be religiously formed, intelligent speakers for Catholicism. Readers in Scripture were appointed, the duties of preachers outlined, the obligation of bishops' residence in their dioceses and their moral and religious competences set forth. Clerical celibacy was upheld, dueling forbidden, and religious orders of men and women reformed. These practical directives eventually issued in the form of a Catechism, a revised Book of Prayer (the Breviary) for clergy and religious, and a Missal and Ritual regulating the sacramental usage of Catholic communities.

Doctrinal decrees on the sacraments, the meaning of the presence of Christ in the Eucharist, Original Sin, marriage and ordination, the authority of the biblical text, and penance were promulgated. In short, there was not a single area of ecclesiastical life that was not touched by the conciliar fathers. They demanded that the theological sources of the Tradition (the Scriptures, earlier doctrinal positions, and medieval Scholasticism without its later accretions) ensure solid but renewed foundations for a reforming community of believers throughout the world. Trent achieved continuity with its past, yet not at the price of repression or separation into fragments.

This stable, uniform culture provided the energy and daring for three extraordinary movements within reforming Catholicism: the rise of activist mystics in Spain; the emergence of the prophetic "armies of God" in the Jesuits, Ursulines, and other local missionaries; and a combination of Church and academy strengthening the revival, indeed, the flowering of Catholicism in the seventeenth and eighteenth centuries.

MYSTICS, MISSIONARIES, AND PERFECT SOCIETIES

What was inaugurated and consolidated by the Council of Trent became much of the substance of the Catholic Church as we have known it prior to Vatican Council II (1962–65). For some 350 years, the art, piety, theology, mysticism, and anti-Protestant polemics of the Catholic Revival marked Christian life. Certainty, caution, and security were the forces at work. It was safer to remain within the fortress of one's Church than to make excursions into theological or religious *terra incognita*. Catholics looked at the splitting seams of the Protestant cloth and huddled triumphantly within the organizational tent of the old renewed Christendom.

Mystics—The Experience of God

In its search for its own origins, the Catholic community focused upon the very religious subjectivity that had animated Luther. In figures like Teresa of Ávila (1515–82) and John of the Cross (1542–91), Catholics maintained that the existential moments of evangelical conversion can and should be found in dialogue with the Tradition. Both figures combined heroic practical sense with shrewd judgment and religious conviction. John's vernacular poetry and theological reflections and Teresa's holy common sense and deep interior life helped form a culture hungering for a language in which to speak of the delicate maneuvers of the spirit in its loving search for God.

Missionaries—The Edges of Ecclesial Life

But the Catholic Revival was meant to convert not the cloistered religious, but the populace. It trained clergy in seminaries, ran schools of religion, gave parochial missions to develop the life of the local community, and established general educational endeavors. Some, especially congregations of women, nursed the sick, founded schools, and performed the charitable and social works left unaccomplished by disbanded or lax monastic communities.

Men and women like Philip Neri (1515–95), Angela de Merici (1474–1540), Francis de Sales (1567–1622), Vincent de Paul (1581–1660), and others cared for pilgrims and convalescents, ministered to galley slaves, founded orphanages, and worked in the local parishes, transforming each particular situation by their charitable, ascetic lives. In their differing ways and cultures, they achieved that personal blend of humanism and Christian grace for which the reforming fathers at Trent had striven. We recognize in Francis de Sales's *Introduction to the Devout Life* not so much austere and grand mystical raptures, but a sure insight into the lives of ordinary men and women. Philip Neri and Vincent de Paul are not fierce and startling prophets, but they remind us that those who dare to become saints need not lose their humanity in the process. When the Revival fostered such domestic virtue, it had succeeded.

But the most notable community of reformers was the Society of Jesus. Ignatius of Loyola (1491/95–1556), its founder, was a military man who, while recuperating from a war wound, experienced a religious conversion. His company of religious soldiers intended to reform the Church internally through education, the frequent use of the sacraments, and missionary preaching. At his death, the Compañia de Jésus extended from Brazil to Japan with over one hundred houses and well over a thousand members. In the chivalrous zeal of Ignatius, Jesuits strove to conquer the world for Christ.

Because their work was always at the edges of ecclesial life, whether in non-European lands (as with Francis Xavier [1506–52] in Sri Lanka, Goa, China, or Japan; with Isaac Jogues [1607–47] among the Hurons and Iroquois of North America, or José de

Anchieta [1553–97] among the Paraguayan Indians) or in polemic disputations with Protestants in Europe, they were always controversial figures. Yet it was not force which succeeded; well-educated teaching and fiery religious preaching were their weapons.

A Perfect Society
One God, One Church, One Culture

If religious fervor was the ultimate origin of the quest for ecclesiastical reform in both its Protestant and Catholic forms, the Catholic community built up its new separated identity through instruments peculiarly its own. By the continued use of Latin in worship, Catholics distinguished their sacred ritual from profane vernacular cultures; nonsacramental devotions, such as the rosary and other private prayers, filled the gap between popular religious instinct and official services. If Protestants would deny the incarnational mediations of Christian faith by an emphasis upon the overpowering graciousness of God, then Catholics would stress the sacramental, ecclesiastical, juridical, hierarchical, and cultural instruments of Divine Presence.

Polemics made Catholic theologians and preachers defensive. Watchdogs of confessional purity, such as the Holy Office (begun 1542) or the Index of Forbidden Books (1557–1966), condemned opinions and made believers cautious. Consolidation of position on the safest territory possible was the plan. Somewhat surprisingly, such strategies produced creative theologies.

In two figures we have a paradigm of this development. Melchior Cano (1509–60), a Spanish Dominican, provided the internal argumentation by which theology was largely known well into this century. Robert Bellarmine (1542–1621) offered a rationale for the structure of the post-Tridentine Church which, with some significant additions, has persisted through the Second Vatican Council.

Cano categorized the various sources of theology (Scripture, Tradition, reason) so that they could be given priority and rank in theological discussion. Appeals to Scripture and Tradition were paramount; then followed the interpretations of the universal Church, councils, decrees of the Roman See, the Fathers, and Scholastics. Only then could one appeal to the "foreign" sources for proof: natural reason, philosophy, historical examples, and personal witness, in descending

89

order of importance. Then the Catholic thinker could make a judgment concerning the certainty or probability of the results, and a pious reflection might be added to aid devotion.

This rather dry formulation was primarily an appeal to authority, which Thomas Aquinas would have thought the weakest link in the chain of religious argument. Cano gave the impression that the truth of Catholic faith could be achieved without reference to believers' conversion in community, their prayer and worship, or their moral authenticity in public life.

What Cano developed for a hierarchical method in theology, Bellarmine offered as a stratified version of the authorities in the Church. Thomas Aquinas could assume a Church with a body of Tradition stretching back to the apostles; for Bellarmine, that was precisely what was contested. Since individuals could now decide whether to belong to the Catholic Church or to a Reformed Tradition, it had become necessary to offer some understanding of Catholicism's legitimacy. What duties were now required of those who belonged? How were we to know the true Church of Christ's Gospel?

Bellarmine provided a solution by maintaining that the Church as a divine gift must necessarily reflect the most perfect of societies—a monarchy. Since it has a single authority, with guaranteed unity of allegiance, uniform adherence, and coherent beliefs, it must be the best of social bodies. The visible society of the Church required just such a central authority to ensure its identity. Catholics could always be marked by their loyalty to this one regime, disclosing their faith among the hostile religious differences of the world. Nonbelievers would always know this group by its universality (catholic), fullness and variety of believers (holy), its strict continuity or succession from the apostles (apostolic), and the uniformity of its members with the pope (one).

Although Bellarmine helpfully categorized ecclesial life in a period of confusion, what disappears from his view are the plural cultures in which Catholics live and work. In emphasizing papal unity, he neglects any semiautonomous agents in the Church (councils, bishops, or theologians) and grants them little influence. In this Church, prophets are not likely to be accepted as authentic speakers of the charisms of the Spirit.

Now by the time this vision of the Church had taken hold in the Catholic community, it only paralleled the experience of absolutism and the divine right of national monarchs. In one sense Bellarmine provided a path by which the Catholic Church could play a social role independent of the civil rulers with whose limitation of the human rights of their subjects it often disagreed. Just as the Christian community had assimilated Jewish presbyteral government, Roman judicial procedures, feudal fealties, and imperial trappings to leave itself room for social independence, so now it began to find its alignment alongside monarchical nation-states.

In each era, however, the Church has always risked losing its identity in the particularities of the period in which it has found itself. That it has not remains a testimony to the dialogue engendered by its prophets and visionaries. With some of those voices now in alternate versions of Christendom, whether at Wittenburg, Utrecht, London, Edinburgh, or Geneva, this self-critical discussion became a rivalry among brothers and sisters, a competition for the testament of a seemingly absent Father. The unfinished conversations of those days continue to plague us.

DANGLING CONVERSATIONS
OF RECONSTITUTED CHRISTENDOMS

Christians of various confessional Traditions are now left with an accumulation of questions which cannot be ignored. What had been open, if contested, issues in a united Church had now become controversial arguments from authority dividing parties and Churches. Questions in one area became suspicions in another. Theologians condemned spiritual enthusiasts; ecclesiastical leaders feared theologians and peasant believers alike; believers thirsted for the Spirit and were afraid of being given a stone by clergy and thinkers together.

Yet in such a thin environment, the Catholic Revival reasserted certain principles of Christian life contravened by the Protestant Reformers. There was an *intrinsic relationship* between God's grace in redemption and the life of God given in creation (humanity was not depraved, but seriously flawed by sin). The sacred and the profane could not be separated as absolutes (government and Church must both reflect evangelical values). And the sacramental life of the Church was an authentic continuation of Christ's redeeming Presence (Christ's gift of the Spirit was a *visible Presence*). The stress on the mediations of God's grace and love was authentically Catholic, a universal remembrance of the Christian Tradition.

But any number of matters were posed and left unanswered or answered too hastily and therefore unsatisfactorily. How is this gift of God's grace stated in a new pluralist cultural situation? How is the Bible at once the Church's book and the religious formation of believers? The Christ-event is surely normative for the entire religious Tradition: social, institutional, and political. How is he also an existential moment in the hearts of believers such that it does not overturn the social government of Christian life? Must the prophetic and traditional always be in opposition?

The problem is that the partners of this dialogue had separated—unwilling to stay in the same room to talk to one another. It is fruitless hindsight to say that had the elements of power and money not been involved, dispassionate conversation might have ensued. That is naive. For Christian discourse is also about fiscal and political economy. The belief of Christians is that they can handle the snakelike social praxis of the world as well as their own interior religious experience. Here both sides failed with disastrous consequences for all. The rare individual in this period who understood all the factors of the disintegrating medieval world, burgeoning early modern polities, and the religious ardor of believers did not often find a conversation partner. Lecturing the Reformers or Catholic Revivalists is condescending; answering their unanswered questions in the present may become a blessing.

ANTICIPATIONS OF A FUTURE WORLD

A final sacrament of the Catholic resolution of religion and culture during this period can be seen in the ambiguous role missionaries played in the expanding European economies and colonial governments. After the Treaty of Tordesillas, administered by Alexander VI (1492–1503), Spanish, Portuguese, and Italian preachers traveled with the military conquerors of each country to Brazil, the Caribbean, Africa, the Far East, and the Americas. Wherever the colonizers ruled, churches were founded, schools were established, even universities (Mexico, 1544) were inaugurated.

The underlying assumption of this colonial missionary effort was that Christendom (whether Spanish, Portuguese, English, Italian, etc.), the best form of religious and political belief, should be given to all. Missionaries baptized entire populations of natives whose understanding and appropriation of Catholicism can have been only minimal at best.

There were exceptions of course—individuals like Bartolomeo de Las Casas (1474–1566), who worked tirelessly against the slave trade, pleading persistently for the equality of the native populations with the Spanish colonizers. An even more stunning example can be found in Mattheo Ricci (1552–1610), Jesuit missionary to China, who spoke and wrote classical Chinese, dressed as a mandarin, learned Asian science, and presented the Christian Gospel as the fulfillment of Confucian wisdom.

What the Jesuits in China understood was that the universality of Catholicism was not an abstract unicultural religious expression. Rather it required accommodation (as they called it) to the indigenous language, mores, and previous beliefs of the people. In this century we find that an enlightened view, but the controversies that it raised in Catholicism were significant. To permit other cultural expressions of Christianity was to admit diversity into the Gospel of Christ. The Gospel of Christ was not to be compromised with the "barbarism" of the "unenlightened."

The fundamental question raised by the Reformers was evangelization. Does the Gospel have only a single cultural shape? Can it be expressed with a range of legitimate doctrinal, ethical, and ecclesiastical positions? Can differing existential embodiments of Christian language, literature, art, and polity subsist side by side without competition, subjugation, mutual syncretism, or bored tolerance?

Where the Christendom of the High Middle Ages had disintegrated into the fragmented Churches of the Reform, whether Catholic or Protestant, each was forced for a time to rethink its identity as *the* authentic heir of the Christian Gospels. Yet when each had strengthened its ecclesiastical bulwarks against external Christian neighbors, it discovered that the pluralism without only registered a pluralism of cultures within the walls. External war had become internal strife.

NOTES

1. French text quoted in Johan Huizinga, *The Waning of the Middle Ages* (Garden City, N.Y.: Doubleday & Co., 1954), 36.

2. "To John Bradaček and the People of Krumlov," in *The Letters of John Hus,* trans. Matthew Spinka (Totowa, N.J.: Rowman and Littlefield, 1972), 53.

3. See Huizinga, *Middle Ages,* 185–86, 315–16.

4. William James, *The Varieties of Religious Experience* (New York: Collier Books, 1961), 242.

5. Edmund Bishop, *Liturgica Historica* (Oxford: At the Clarendon Press, 1962), 449–50.

6. *Little Sermons on Sin. The Archpriest of Talavera,* trans. Lesley Byrd Simpson (Berkeley and Los Angeles: University of California Press, 1977), 158.

7. Hilaire Belloc, *Europe and the Faith* (New York: Paulist, 1930), 211.

8. *Fidei Ratio* (1530), excerpted in *Documents Illustrative of the Continental Reformation,* ed. B. J. Kidd (Oxford: At the Clarendon Press, 1911), 474.

9. Norman Cohn, *The Pursuit of the Millennium: Revolutionary Messianism in Medieval and Reformation Europe and its Bearing on Modern Totalitarian Movements* (New York: Harper & Row, 1961), 256.

FURTHER RELATED MATERIAL

No one reads quickly through the Reformation. Josef Lortz's important study, *The Reformation in Germany* (New York: Herder & Herder, 1968) is in two volumes, but crucial. Less demanding surveys can be found in Owen Chadwick, *The Reformation* (Baltimore: Penguin Books, 1964); John Dolan, *The History of the Reformation* (New York: Mentor-Omega, 1967); and Steven Ozment, *The Age of Reform: 1250–1550: An Intellectual and Religious History of Late Medieval and Reformation Europe* (New Haven: Yale University Press, 1980). For descriptions of the final period of medieval decline, see the entertaining, if somewhat depressing, Johan Huizinga, *The Waning of the Middle Ages,* (Garden City, N.Y.: Doubleday & Co., 1954). On the Catholic Revival, see A. G. Dickens, *The Counter Reformation* (New York: Harcourt Brace Jovanovich, 1969) and J. C. Olin, *The Catholic Reformation: Savanarola to Ignatius Loyola; Reform in the Church, 1495–1540* (New York: Harper & Row, 1969).

8

CATHOLIC ISOLATIONISM: THE ALTERNATE CULTURE (1630–1789)

> But reverend discipline, and religious fear,
> And soft obedience, find sweet biding here;
> Silence and sacred rest, peace and pure joys,
> Kind loves keep house, lie close, and make noise,
> And room enough for monarchs, while none swells
> Beyond the kingdoms of contentful cells.
> > Richard Crashaw (1613–49), from "Description
> > of a Religious House and Condition of Life."

When Ulrich Zwingli (1484–1531), the Swiss Reformer, visited the pilgrimage Church of Einsiedeln, he was shocked at its trivializing levity and superstition. Less than two hundred years later, Caspar Moosbrugger (1656–1723), an art-loving brother of the same monastic community, designed (1719–23) a decorated Baroque masterpiece to enshrine Catholic triumph. As one enters the square, the grand scale and palatial character of the façade displays itself chastely in gray-green stone. But upon entering the octagon which begins the nave, the believer is captured by the elaborate ornament and stunning frescoes completed by the Asam brothers (Cosmos, 1686–1739, and Egid, 1692–1750).

The viewer makes common cause with what seems to be a fellow pilgrim looking into the dome, his stucco foot firmly planted on the very top of a pillar. What the supplaint sees is an uncountable multitude of earlier believers: shepherds and sheep, angels and saints in the open air, spiraling toward the manger in Bethlehem. Above this incarnation, in the center, is the Father of Lights—located in the intensely serene brightness of eternity.

Catholic baroque art stressed the unity of earth and heaven. The believers' faith draws them from what is seen to the Unseen, from the heard to the Unheard, from what is tangible to the God who always escapes human grasp. These monuments present a regularly placid (occasionally stolidly triumphal) face to the world—yet entrance into their space proclaims a power not their own, seducing the believer through sheer multiplicity of detail into a rapture of divine love.

The conspicuous contrast reflects the life of seventeenth- and eighteenth-century Catholicism. The problems caused by the Reformers were by the 1700s largely internalized, not solved. Controversy had made the Church prudent in securing a seemly façade; the discussions of Catholic piety, theology, and discipline took place behind closed doors whenever possible. The marketplace was neglected.

Isolated by political power when hegemony in Europe passed to the northern countries, Catholicism began to turn Roman insularity from an external requirement into a cultural policy. The once vibrant Catholic spirit neglected, even opposed at times, the rise of the European scientific spirit. To be "enlightened" did not mean to be baptized as it once had, but to be free of authoritative, ready-made religious solutions. Catholic intellectuals retreated into narrower familial concerns without prophecy, without vision.

A historian of cultures might view such a withdrawal as a necessary stage in the recurring cycles of all religious development. Just as it is essential for the individual to return to the affective comfort of family and friends to restore energy and accept healing for the larger tasks of work, country, and society, so too Catholicism required a retreat. But the creative, even daring, approaches which Catholicism brought to its former situations contrasted sharply with the parochial views which developed from the end of the Thirty Years War (1648) until the French Revolution (1789).

During this phase Catholicism seemed to be more defensive, less secure than at any time in its past. Despite the Baroque ornamental devices, Catholic portraits appeared somewhat drab and lackluster. But the Church was not without its prophets and saints or its moments of beauty and valor. In providing an alternate culture to the more powerful outside world, it produced a set piece which has lasted well into this century.

THE CRISES WITHIN

Gallicanism

France, proud of its title "eldest daughter of the church," tenaciously, even brutally, held to its religious identity when its powerful neighbors had turned to the Protestant Reform. When Jacques Bossuet (1627–1704), the great court preacher and bishop, wrote his *Discourse on Universal History* (1681) for Louis XIV (1643–1715), he pressed the specifically religious claims made by God on rulers of nations.

> They neither control the configuration of circumstances that was bequeathed to them by past centuries, nor can they foresee the course of the future, much less control that course. All this is in the hands of Him Who can name what is and what is yet to be, Who presides over all the ages, and Who knows in advance what will come to pass.[1]

Nonetheless, Louis XIV used the Catholic Church as a substantial cannon in the French arsenal of political independence, authority, and power.

This political union of Catholicism and French national interest provoked the first great internal crisis during this period. Labeled Gallicanism, it revealed French pretensions to, and accomplishment of, an international hegemony. For many centuries, to be "civilized" meant to speak, write, and (often enough) think French thoughts. When the political centralization of Louis XIV's power turned to religious matters, it expressed itself in the affirmation by the French clergy (at the instigation and support of Bossuet) of the *Four Gallican Articles* (1682). They asserted that the king, not the pope, had authority in civil affairs and that general councils must consent to, or deny, contested papal judgments. Although the *Articles* were denied by Pope Alexander VIII (1689–91) in 1690 and retracted by the king himself in 1693, they were taught and promulgated in France for a decade. The question of the rights and privileges of the French national church continued to bedevil theological and political interchange for almost a century.

What remains distressing about such in-house investigations is that they diverted the best minds of the era into problems more ecclesiastical than theological. Studies into the nature of the Church's evangelical role in the wider world and the implications of justification and grace for society were shunted to one side, while interminable arguments took place concerning the appointment of French bishops and the administration of theological seminaries. There is little doubt that Gallicanism intensified French Catholics' temptation toward cultural withdrawal. The twentieth-century loss of the "working-class Catholic" in France has its origins much earlier than this era.

Jansenism

Simultaneously, a graver, more lasting internal debate appeared in the form of Jansenism. Named after Cornelius Jansen (1585–1638), a professor at the University of Louvain in Belgium, the movement focused French discussion upon a significant, if probably insoluble, theological issue. It reopened the Church's reflections on the nature of justification: "How is the Christian saved by God in Christ?"

Jansen returned to Augustine for his answers; and, in a lengthy, posthumously published text (the *Augustinus,* 1642), he defended what he believed to be the Bishop of Hippo's position. Most would now agree that Jansen was neither entirely faithful to his mentor nor to the difficulty of the problem itself. He gave such an exclusive prominence to God's activity in every action that the reality of human freedom was placed in jeopardy.

It is not likely that this question will ever be completely resolved. The *Decree on Justification* from the Council of Trent asserted that God's loving grace is always a gift, always prior to our own acceptance—but that our acceptance is also always and in all ways free. Theologians realize that this *is* the mystery of divine-human interaction—and that to locate the disclosure of the gift is the fundamental task, not to *explain* the event exhaustively. But theologians always have a tendency to want to unpuzzle the world, just the way any thinker does—and Jansen was no exception.

Jansen's French followers were determined to reform ecclesiastical life. They were keen, ambitious, subtle, and stubborn, convinced that any yielding to human ability in this matter was tantamount to blasphemy. In 1643, Antoine Arnauld (1612–1694), a priest of the community of Port-Royal near Paris, wrote a small text, *On Frequent Communion,* which severely criticized the practice, emphasizing the sinfulness of believers and their need for the correct interior dispositions to be truly Christian. On the one hand, Arnauld's practices fostered a prophetic grasp of the reality of the gracious God in an authentically Christian life; on the other, they favored a gloomy, austere opinion of human possibilities and a distrust of the ordinary sacramental life of believers.

The result was a division of French Catholicism into Jansenists and more traditional Catholics led by the Jesuits. Some, like Molière (1622–73) in his play *Le Tartuffe* (1669), satirized religious pessimism and false asceticism. But the Jansenists had a literate sympathizer in Blaise Pascal (1623–62), who was both repelled by the superficiality of Catholic textbook morality and attracted to the severe demands of Jansenist piety.

In the *Provincial Letters* (1656–57), Pascal exposed the immorality of simplistic ethical complacency and caricatured Jansenism's opponents. So brilliant were his polemics and his literary style as a controversialist that European Jesuits remained stigmatized as dangerous laxists and devious politicians.

The religious fervor of Jansenism did not last. Because its legacy was not the joyful experience of Francis of Assisi, the activist piety of Teresa of Ávila, or the benign wisdom of Philip Neri, it could not be successful in its attempts to reform Catholic morals. On the contrary, Jansenism's negative tone gave the very word "Jansenist" the popular meaning of a narrow moralism peculiar to certain Catholic populations. Cornelius Jansen, Blaise Pascal, and many others strove to be prophets; but the Jansenist Catholics peopling the novels of François Mauriac and Graham Greene regularly witness to a more defeatist vision of human nature.

Quietism

If Jansenist asceticism promoted a task-oriented religiosity, Quietism did the precise opposite. The founder, Miguel de Molinos (1628–96), recommended in his *Spiritual Guide* (1675) that the religious individual must achieve the silence of complete contemplation, even at the price of annihilating personal projects, ritual and ascetic practices, or resistance to temptation itself. The soul must be indifferent to everything but God.

Molinos's stress upon the terrifying and fascinating call to holiness (*Mysterium tremendum et fascinans*) captured the fervor of many contemplative women whose spiritual lives he directed. When these religious sisters discarded their private devotions, refused to recite public prayer, and generally disturbed discipline in their communities, Molinos was condemned. Throughout the process of imprisonment, trial, and judgment, Molinos remained submissive and undisturbed.

Molinos's doctrine spread to France through the conferences and letters of Jeanne Marie de la Motte-Guyon (1648–1717), who taught that believers must cultivate complete indifference toward God, excluding even the thought of reward or punishment. Upon meeting her in 1688, François de Salignac de la Mothe Fénélon (1641–1715), archbishop of Cambrai, missionary to French Protestants, and tutor to the grandson of Louis XIV, began a long controversy with Bossuet on the questions of grace, free will, and the interior life of the spiritual person. Bossuet somewhat peevishly accused Fénélon of being an enthusiast, little better than a heretic. After a bitter quarrel, Roman authorities intervened at the king's request. Fénélon's positions were termed rash and liable to cause scandal. The archbishop acquiesed without reservation.

By emphasizing the demands of God's invitation, Quietism deepened the Catholic Revival at a time when the European Church required considerable religious conversion; but its attack on public activity of all kinds encouraged the same withdrawal from broader cultural pursuits that Gallicanism invited and Jansenism supported. These prophetically inspired movements could not reform a Catholicism which further divided itself in self-examination.

Politics

By order of the Queen Mother of France, Catherine de' Medici (1519–89), well over five thousand Protestants were slaughtered on St. Bartholomew's Eve (24 August 1572). It was only a symbol of the civil and theological battles undertaken by bishops, kings, and assembly to secure an absolutely integral national identity and to suppress religious diversity. In England, the national or Anglican church (1533), initiated by Henry VIII (1491–1547) to establish his Tudor dynasty and consolidated under Elizabeth I (1533–1603), tolerated a range of religious expression which erupted into civil war (1642–48) between Anglican Royalists and Puritan Roundheads under the leadership of Oliver Cromwell (1599–1658).

But in Germany the savage Thirty Years' War (1618–48) pillaged and depopulated entire independent principalities. French political strategy continuously encouraged the intervention of foreign mercenaries, turning a weak neighbor into a limping enemy.

During these wars, Catholic and Protestant ecclesiastics fought for control of old territorial boundaries through the military remainders of their dynastic, familial, and political ambitions. The Peace of

Westphalia (1648) ended the war, returned property rights of both parties to 1618, balanced imperial electors between Catholics and Lutherans, and granted mutual toleration and political equality to all parties. No one was satisfied, and neither religious group could claim anything but a worried, bored exhaustion.

After the Peace of Westphalia, German Catholics strengthened the revival of their religion in their own lands. Popes of the period shifted support among kings and emperors to achieve political leverage and support for Catholics in the civil wars in the north. When the popes' civil power declined, they were obliged to attend to their ecclesiastical possessions in Italy (the Papal States) as a way of preserving their own independence. Even though their moral authority increased, due to the election of worthier candidates, they found themselves capable only of inviting or persuading civil powers to participate in political quarrels.

THE CRISIS WITHOUT

The self-isolation and insulation by others of Catholic piety, political identity, and theology made the Church particularly unprepared to face the most important moments of the early modern world. If the plunder of buildings, the wounds of war, and the snatching at sterile authority seemed to be the immediate problems to be healed and restored, the long view of Catholic identity required that more patient, more attentive medicine be given to the discoveries of modern science and the surgeries wrought by the Enlightenment.

Revolutionary Science

The English historian Herbert Butterfield has remarked that the scientific revolution "outshines everything since the rise of Christianity and reduces the Renaissance and Reformation to the rank of mere episodes, mere internal displacements, within the system of medieval Christendom."[2] As Butterfield phrases the matter, picturesquely but accurately, this new mode of Western thought required people to don new thinking caps.

We have grown so accustomed to our scientific garments that we forget how truly novel they were in the European world. The epic adventure of modern science controverted the geopolitical centrism of the European West, overturned Aristotelian physics as its normative self-explanation, and reexamined, then discarded, large elements of the culture formed from Greco-Roman and ancient Hebrew ingredients. If we are to understand ourselves in the present or appreciate the vast difference modern science brought to all religious traditions, including the Catholic one, we must understand the nature of this contemporary journey.

Galileo Galilei

The easiest way to convey the difference between the old and the new attitudes toward the experience of our world is to focus upon the melancholy tale of Galileo Galilei (1564–1642) and his tangled relationship with the Church at Rome. In Padua, where he taught for eighteen years, Galileo improved the telescope and revolutionized astronomy, leading him to agree with the theories of Copernicus (1473–1543), who had hypothesized that the earth moved about the sun. For Copernicus, this theory best explained the data of variations in seasons, the movement of the planets, and other astronomical phenomena. Galileo, with his telescope, provided the empirical evidence for the claims—and it is this which placed him in contest with the Roman Inquisition.

Galileo was forbidden to teach or defend the Copernican position because it was "philosophically foolish and preposterous and, because contrary to Scripture, theologically heretical." Galileo kept silent for a time (some fifteen years), but shortly before his death he spoke again and was condemned.

Galileo's insistence upon a new method lay at the heart of the seventeenth-century conflict between religion and science. Religious thinkers of that time knew only two major approaches to the question of truth: the *authoritative* (i.e., God's Word in the Scriptures and the Tradition of the Church) and the *philosophical* (i.e., the largely deductive, metaphysical methods of Greek philosophers and medieval Scholastics). To argue for an *experimentally rigorous verifiable method* was a radical departure; it struck a major blow at the intellectual certitudes of the day.

Galileo's "compositive" and "resolutive" method (as he called it) was not, however, a mere piling up of particulars. Rather he argued from mathematical hypotheses through verifying experiments. It was his belief that mathematics analyzed the very structure of things; to be scientific was to be in contact with what was real. This shift in empirical seeing, inductive thinking, in experimental knowing itself, was intensified when the results called into question not only the received natural science of the ancients (Ptolemy [the second-century C.E. Greco-Egyptian astronomer] and Aristotle), but even the view of the world held through the prevailing literalist understanding of the Scriptures.

The Inquisition's triumph over Galileo (only examined by the Roman Curia again in our times) was a Pyrrhic victory. Not only were Galileo's methods valid and his scientific conclusions vindicated, but all attempts to contain the empirical method only isolated the Catholic Church further from future intellectual currents.

What so frightened the religious officials of Galileo's day can now be seen as a complicated question, but a false dilemma. Science as a careful, empirical, inductive, and verifiable procedure is a sure way of discovering the truth about reality. Religion, disclosing the ultimate meanings of our human experience, remains the surest way to embody, apprehend, and understand the *limits of* all reality and the *limits to* all possible experience. Contemporary scientists and religious believers understand and accept what could not be seen three hundred years ago: that there need be no real clash between authentic science and authentic religion.

Blaise Pascal

Pascal's (1623–62) preeminence is not due to his literary abilities in the Jansenist crisis but rather to his capacity for combining mathematical skills and religious fervor. The reader of his *Pensées* (1670) can recognize a transparently honest spirit caught between the two contending factions of his (and his age's) life—science and religion. He was unwilling to forego either, wishing to remain faithful to the scientific methods of his day, while reminding his contemporaries that "the heart has its reasons which reason knows not at all." Wisdom sees the brilliance (*éclat*) and the reverence (*vénération*) due to both Archimedes and Jesus Christ.[3]

Pascal might have found a way to transform the tensions between science and religion into a new cultural synthesis; but the incontrovertible fact is that few listened. As a result, the continued conflicts forced men and women to choose sides; rarely was it possible to achieve both an authentic scientific attitude and continue within a personal confessional Tradition. In the many grand "ifs" of history, we may wonder what Catholic history "might have been" had it been able to heed the thinking of such eminent Catholics *and* scientists.

The Enlightenment—The Rise of Rational Religion

What was in the seventeenth century a movement of scientists, a theoretic method, and a set of practical procedures printed a cultural currency of uncertain denominations for the eighteenth century. Religious insecurities and a general skepticism toward authority, rhetorically inflated during the religious wars, funded attempts to bank religion and culture on reason rather than *any* contentious religious Tradition.

The Enlightenment, as Immanuel Kant (1724–1804) summarized it at the end of the century (1784), was our release from "self-incurred tutelage"—the willingness to become autonomous, leaving behind authorities of religious or cultural dogma and claiming personal freedom. It was a moral ideal of knowledge. To be free risks stepping away from our cherished, self-supported beliefs and to test their meaning and truth by the experiments of reason.

So the Enlightenment concerned itself with the various authorities which required reexamination: *textual authority* like the Scriptures; *confessional Traditions* like Lutheranism or Catholicism; *philosophical assumptions* and *principles* like those of Aristotle; and finally *religion* itself. There was science and there was superstition: the first was critical; the second mere belief, general consent, and tired custom—the authority of the masses.

Kant prodded:

> It is so easy not to be of age. If I have a book which understands for me, a pastor who has a conscience for me, a physician who decides my diet, and so forth, I need not trouble myself. I need not think, if I can only *pay*—others will readily undertake the irksome *work* for me.[4]

Dispassionate Enlightenment would demystify priestcraft and superstition, political tyranny and personal illusion. Reason should triumph.

Textual Slavery

The conflicts over how to read the Bible began when Richard Simon (1638–1712) published his *Critical History of the Old Tes-*

tament (1678). Whether the book was the *Iliad* or the *Pentateuch,* the analysis of the genuine, "critical" text was the same. Simon carefully and simply (in French rather than Latin) showed how the biblical text was altered over the centuries by various authors and later scribes.

Though Simon wished to show Protestants how the Tradition of a text was essential for validation of the Word of God, he ended by calling into question the authenticity of the Hebrew, and later the Christian, Scriptures. The "authority" of superstition would be overcome by sheer attention to the certain facts of the biblical text.

Reaction was swift. Simon was expelled from his religious community, his book banned by the French Royal Council, then later (1683) placed upon the *Index of Forbidden Books.* Bossuet, ever ready to take on controversy, argued in his *History of the Variations of Protestant Churches* (1688) that authority was the only true principle upon which Church could be based. The constantly splitting sects of non-Roman confessions were not simply due to matters of taste, but to a shift from the very unified essence of Christianity itself.

Political Infamy

But European consciousness was changing. Difference was no longer automatic heterodoxy from the received, authentic religious identity; pluralism could be enriching. Believing what one was told without examination was not the ideal. Nowhere can this doctrine be seen more clearly than in that figure who dominated the French Enlightenment, the extraordinary François Marie Arouet (1694–1778), whose pseudonym was Voltaire.

Voltaire is no unworthy exemplar of the entire age. He combined all the virtues and all the limitations of an exciting period. He was witty, polished, liberal, antiecclesiastical. As an author, he is now remembered for his *Candide* (1759), a satirical description of the classical metaphysician's "best of all possible worlds." As a counselor and *philosophe,* he argued for freedom and justice in a world still largely enslaved politically and ideologically.

But this giant of literature, art, and religious toleration also displayed some of the least attractive qualities of the times: an enormous vanity; a failure to separate the abuses of Catholicism from its

105

religious values; and an inability to distinguish between wholesale attack on religious institutions and their gradual, careful reform. He praised the Quakers and Unitarians, but the first for their pacifism, the second for their rationality. The true value of religion was its anticipation of reason. "Every sensible man, every honorable man, must hold the Christian sect in horror."[5]

Since atheism seemed only to beget societal confusion, Voltaire encouraged a minimal loyalty to the religion of reason—Deism. In this intellectual surrogate for confessional Traditions, God appeared as a classic watchmaker who wound up the spring of the machine, set the whole world ticking, and then remained absent in the background without intervention in free human affairs. Christians, protesting Catholics maintained, could not accept *this* God as their own.

Religious Serfdom

Thomas Paine (1737–1809) combined pamphlets in favor of revolutionary independence from the King of England with rational freedom from religious subservience. In *Common Sense* (1776) he argued that though we are all "children of the same family," God wills that there should be a diversity of religious opinions among us.[6] Any priestcraft which counters the ideals of the French Revolution had to be destroyed, announced *The Age of Reason* (1793).

A publicist rather than an original thinker, Paine composed direct prose which addressed ordinary individuals. It frightened many; it exhilarated others. Though Jesus was a virtuous and amiable individual, it was curious to Paine that the Christian Church could so easily spring from pagan myth.

> A direct incorporation took place in the first instance, by making the reputed founder to be celestially begotten. The trinity of gods that then followed was no other than a reduction of the former plurality. . . . But when . . . one part of God is represented by a dying man, and another part, called the Holy Ghost, by a flying pigeon,[7]

our credulity is stretched beyond limit. Christianity can only be an "engine of power" by which avaricious priests enslave people through their appeal to a derogatory notion of divinity.

Paine's opposition to religious confessions, however, was due not simply to their overweening authority, but also to their method of theological thought. It was not scientific; it had no data; it demonstrated no conclusions. It is the "study of nothing." Science and religion cannot share the same bed.

A God who encouraged human freedom combined with a strong skepticism concerning the miraculous content of revealed religion made Deism a haven for those, like Voltaire and Paine, who believed that social anarchy would ensue under later materialist thinkers like Denis Diderot (1713–84), Jean le Rond d'Alembert (1717–83), or Paul-Henri d'Holbach (1723–89). Deism, a kind of civil religion, provided distance from historical religious expressions, left the authority of religion to survive in the individual intellect, and offered flexible standards for judging ecclesiastical expressions. It may well be true, as recent interpreters maintain, that the religious instincts of Voltaire and his colleagues were not as nonexistent as some of their opponents would have us believe. It is no less true, however, that the reckless and corrosive nature of their "enlightened" criticism succeeded in separating true religion from true science for several hundred years.

A Plea for Tolerance

Gotthold Ephraim Lessing (1729–82), the most representative figure of the German Enlightenment, became librarian to the Duke of Brunswick at Wolffenbüttel and began to publish fragments of an unpublished work by Hermann Samuel Reimarus (+1769). Reimarus's attacks on scriptural events (the Exodus, the resurrection narratives, etc.) and his plea for tolerance of the Deists encouraged Lessing to appeal to an inner truth which undergirded all specific confessional beliefs. "The written traditions must be interpreted by their inward truth and no written traditions can give the religion any inward truth if it has none."[8]

Lessing's allegiance to religion was more a faith in inner religious optimism. It is "enough if men hold on to Christian love; what happens to the Christian religion does not matter." In *Nathan the Wise* (1779), the protagonist of the drama appeals for tolerance of all religious differences. Jews, Moslems, and Christians are each partial realizations of the one religious truth that exceeds each historical form. Only through common suffering and dialogue will the characters learn their universal humanity. "Now, let each one emulate the other, in affection untouched by prejudice."

Authority stultifies; authority destroys independence; authority, whether in Scripture (with Simon, Paine, and Lessing), in politics, (with Paine and Voltaire), or in religion itself requires criticism. It demands the autonomous mind of the selfless investigator who is willing to weigh all possible evidence and judge for himself or herself. In such a world, born of the scientific revolution, tolerance of difference was crucial; intolerance, bred by the fissiparous politics of religious wars, had only grown into an inhuman ogre whose existence in fairy tales could be fantasized, but whose cancerous existence in the body of the nascent culture must be excised.

CATHOLIC THEOLOGY
AND THE MANUALS OF CERTITUDE

Catholics read the relentless attacks of Voltaire or Paine and the more gentle remonstrances of Lessing with the eyes of those seeking certitude, assured and secure in their own religious political positions. Questions produced doubts; doubts, divisions. And although some rulers, notably the Empress Maria Theresa (1740–80) and her son Joseph II (1780–90), administered ecclesiastical and educational reforms in their Catholic realms, the Church retreated further into a ghetto.

Doctrinal orthodoxy was pronounced in orotund rhetorical tones based upon a textbook theology which distilled into clear, distinct conclusions an essentialist Catholicism. Such analyses ordinarily began not with a question (as in Aquinas), but with a position, a thesis. One defined its terms, indicated the status of the proposition (of defined faith, only proximate to faith, etc.), noted any adversaries, and then proved the thesis by appeal to specific texts of Scripture, the Tradition, and correlative doctrines. Theology was a proof for the already-held doctrines of belief.

In ethical analysis, Catholic consciences were formed according to the established principles, customs, and rules of belief. It was an ethics of obedience in which no one should act without certainty of motive or the objective knowledge of the good. Ambiguity was to be avoided at all costs. Elaborate rules of discernment which helped the believer to establish the most probable authority were developed. And in Catholic seminaries, endless cases were presented to prepare future priests for all the possibilities in which principles might be contravened.

This formal theological organization held sway in Catholic seminaries well into the twentieth century. It emphasized certainty, universality, abstract reason, and propositional knowledge. But the high degree of abstraction, the controversies within theological circles, and the rigorist doctrinal and ethical positions left the mass of the Catholic population largely untouched. Since theology did not function as an engaged critique of the symbolic, gestural, and ethical lives of Catholics, it is not surprising that the proponents of Jansenist or Quietist piety were successful.

But the disparity between popular piety and theological criticism is in many ways a direct product of the years of the Reformation. The emphasis by the Reformers on the clarity and integrity of the Word of God and their relative disapproval of medieval sacramental life produced a reaction in Catholic life. On the one hand, there was a constant stress on the visual, sacramental aspects of ecclesial life; on the other, a deliberate attention to the catechetical instruction and doctrinal purity of believers. The Enlightenment milieu fostered further refinements in propositional form; and reformed religion, whether Catholic or Protestant, became largely an elitist affair.

So just as an almost Cartesian (after René Descartes, the philosopher, 1596–1650) theology survived into this century, so too did Catholics stress dependence upon papal authority as the primary formation of conscience, the extrasacramental piety of novenas in honor of particular saints as models of behavior, parochial missions or revivals, a growing devotion concerning Mary, the Mother of God, and an emphasis upon the adoration of the reserved Presence of Christ in the Eucharistic Bread.

These developing sensibilities were the popular Catholic response to the failure of theologians, Catholic philosophers, and institutional representatives to wrestle more creatively and more tellingly with the giants of early modern science and Enlightenment. For the modern meaning of Catholicism is as much a product of ordinary Catholic believers as of an institutional Tradition.

Separated by a strictly Catholic culture, insulated from the ever-widening circles of attack, Catholics could better negotiate some inner peace—but a religious peace bought at a level of religious coinage which contemporary believers find largely uninteresting and at a price which made their currency unusable in the rapidly changing world. Private piety and public isolation did not ready the Catholic opera of sensibilities to greet the revolutions of the late eighteenth century.

REVOLUTION AGAINST RIGIDITY—1789

The attacks of the Enlightenment philosophers upon the political and religious tradition were largely intellectual, since it was not until the end of the eighteenth century that the Age of Enlightenment gave way to an Age of Revolution. Inspired by the revolt of the British colonies in America (1775–83) and by Enlightenment critiques of monarchical injustices, the French raised the standard of full and complete revolution (1789) against their hierarchical society. The story of this monumental shift in society is best told in a history other than a chronicle of Catholicism, but the Church was deeply affected by its results.

Catholics fell on both sides of this greatest of divides. For those who chose support of the revolutionaries, this was a providential event. So determined had the most "Catholic" of monarchs been to extend his absolute and "divine" power to the lives of his subjects that the Church itself was seriously weakened and in many ways was subjected to the crown's whims. In such a situation many agreed with the anonymous French observer who wrote: "God saved the Church by sending the French Revolution to destroy princely absolutism." But most official Catholic representatives could not greet the revolution and its demands with anything but horror and condemnation.

So began one of the most critical struggles in the self-understanding of Catholicism. On the one side stood those revolutionary Catholics who accepted even the brutal, violent history of the age as an instance of God's judgment upon the rulers of their society and as an opportunity for human beings to link the battle for freedom with the quest for universal love. It would presage a new

Catholic Revival, a cultivation of democratic community. On the other side, there converged the "conservative" forces of Catholicism, already exhausted by internal crises and external battles with "godless" science and the vultures of the Enlightenment. Their solution was to retreat further into Catholic culture, the perfect society with its clear and distinct truths, its absolute moral rules, and its sure authoritarian political structure. Even though the initial promise of the French Revolution disintegrated rapidly into the despotisms of violence, war, and the Napoleonic order, the Catholic Church of the nineteenth century remained polarized between these progressive and conservative parties. The questions raised by the Reform concerning individual piety and personal conscience, by science and its quest for an empirical validity of knowledge, and by the Enlightenment on the philosophical value of historical differences would not be ignored.

NOTES

1. Jacques-Bénigne Bossuet, *Discourse on Universal History,* trans. Elborg Forster, ed. Orest Ranum (Chicago: University of Chicago Press, 1976), 375.

2. Herbert Butterfield, *The Origins of Modern Science, 1300–1800* (New York: Free Press, 1966), 7.

3. Blaise Pascal, *Pensées* XII, 793, in *Pensées et Opuscules,* ed. Leon Brunschvicg (Paris: Hachette, 1971), 696–97.

4. Immanuel Kant, "What is Enlightenment?" in *History,* trans. Lewis White Beck, Robert E. Anchor, and Emil Fackenheim (Indianapolis: Bobbs-Merrill, 1963), 3.

5. Peter Gay, *The Enlightenment: An Interpretation. The Rise of Modern Paganism* (New York: Vintage, 1968), 391.

6. Thomas Paine, *Common Sense,* ed. Nelson F. Adkins (Indianapolis: Bobbs-Merrill, 1953), 41.

7. Thomas Paine, *The Age of Reason* (Secaucus, N.J.: Citadel, 1974), 53–55, 187.

8. G. E. Lessing, *Lessing's Theological Writings,* trans. Henry Chadwick (Stanford, Calif.: Stanford University Press, 1957), 15–18.

FURTHER RELATED MATERIAL

For a general introduction to this complex political period, see Gerald R. Cragg, *The Church and the Age of Reason, 1648–1789* (Baltimore: Penguin Books, 1966). Ronald Knox's sometimes slanted book *Enthusiasm: A Chap-*

ter in the History of Religion with Special Reference to the Seventeenth and Eighteenth Centuries (New York: Oxford University Press, 1961) is still useful for recapturing the flavor of popular religion. Paul Hazard's *The European Mind, 1680–1715,* trans. J. Lewis May (Harmondsworth, Eng.: Penguin Books, 1973) offers the classic intellectual overview of the shifting consciousness of the period. Peter Gay's *The Enlightenment: An Interpretation—The Rise of Modern Paganism* (New York: Vintage, 1968) outlines the more important figures. For the best overview of the rise of modern scientific method and its consequences, see Herbert Butterfield, *The Origins of Modern Science, 1300–1800* (New York: Free Press, 1966).

9

THE CHALLENGE OF HISTORY (1800–1900)

Oh, what a shifting parti-color'd scene
Of hope and fear, of triumph and dismay
Of recklessness and penitence, has been
The history of that dreary, life-long fray!
John Henry Newman (1801–1890),
from "The Dream of Gerontius"

Igor Stravinsky (1882–1971), composer and conductor, locates the change from Johann Sebastian Bach (1685–1750) to Richard Wagner (1813–83) in the experience of dissonance.[1] In Bach the music regularly resolves its dissonant, clashing sounds into the peace of harmonic order; in Wagner dissimilar tones emancipate themselves, thrust their harsh distensions independently toward the ear, grip the listener with at once a nostalgia for the old repose and a yearning for some future musical meaning. The transcendent became no longer the symmetrical arrangement of parts in an architectural whole, but the concurrence of discrete individuals jostling for simultaneous unity.

At the beginning of the nineteenth century, music still fit the old forms, but at its conclusion, musical form itself became a problem. Opera no longer fit the stage of its origins, symphonies sounded formless to the uneducated ear, and sonatas became the irregular, effusive phantasies of the composer. Musical pieces required larger complements of instruments, orchestras became bigger and louder, performances reached for more populous audiences.

Catholic identity underwent just such a transformation. The interwoven texture of melodic individuals, the instruments of communication, and the counterpoint to the political difficulties of the era originally seemed to fit within the old, rigorously formal shapes of ecclesiastical life. After the French Revolution (1789) and its initial shock to the Church's too easy liaison with monarchical or imperial absolutists, the clashing strains provoked the institution to return to its old nostalgic harmonies.

The major and minor conflicts that compose nineteenth-century Catholic experience lead directly to our contemporary problems. What had once in the eighteenth century been an angry attack by those outside the community upon those inside its walls became a duel within the ecclesiastical house itself. There were those who labeled themselves "liberals." They believed that it was possible to include the Reformers' notions of religious experience, the scientists' methods of knowing, and the philosophers' invitation to tolerance and political freedom within the Church without destroying it. But those who called themselves "conservatives" heard no hope of internal harmony, convinced the newer distensions were only the old heretical ones. Let us briefly examine this contrast through two important instances: *The Syllabus of Errors* (1864) and the journal *L'Avenir* (*The Future*), published by Felicité Robert de Lamennais (1782–1854).

In the *Syllabus,* we have an example of the flight from the contemporary world advocated by some conservative ecclesiastics. It stated that the Roman pontiff need not reconcile himself to "progress, liberalism, and modern civilization." In eighty propositions, it condemned all the movements contemporaries thought forward-thinking. It epitomized in its ill-fated tone a peculiar characteristic of the century's expression of Catholicism.

In previous chapters, we have traced traditional, prophetic, and apocalyptic strands of the Catholic Church in a variety of different ways. During these troubled years a strange blending of the traditional and the apocalyptic took place, evidenced in many of the official documents of the Church such as the *Syllabus.* "Conservatism," in its best sense, draws strength for the present from its memories of God's actions. It conserves and preserves the cognitive, ethical, and affective center of what religious men and women have experienced in their heritage. But during this century conservatives did not merely remember creatively, they judged and often condemned what did not fit their notion of Tradition.

The first half of the century appeared to hold better hopes. De Lamennais and the journal *L'Avenir* crusaded for an alliance between the Church and democratic freedom. He preached a society in which liberties of speech, press, and religion would guarantee the necessary Catholic principle of freedom. These "pilgrims of God and

114

liberty" (as they called themselves) supported the growing revolutionary movements in Europe (Belgium and Poland), and warned that union of Church and state was not necessarily in believers' best interests.

De Lamennais's pleas went unheard. Successive papal decrees in the 1830s told Polish, Belgian, and Irish Catholics to support their local Protestant governments. De Lamennais's own positions were officially rejected in 1832. While the popes frequently intervened in local disputes in place of lower authorities, they sought "balance" between the competing factors in political problems. This search for balance regularly placed the administrative authority not so much in creative response to past traditions but in a simple repetition for the sake of future preservation. Balance, though often our common-sense method for handling ordinary affairs, is simply insufficient as a Gospel response to civil and religious crisis.

Catholic theological and ecclesiastical oscillations in the nineteenth century do not make easy reading. Despite political complexities which lasted through the dissolution of the Papal States (1870), there were public signs of a future Church struggling to enter the twentieth century. Indeed some of the movements, such as the revival of Thomas Aquinas, which struck contemporaries as repetitions of the past, actually helped Peter's alternately enthusiastic and lukewarm Church lurch its way into the modern world.

FACING THE MODERN WORLD

Preliminaries: Hume and Kant

The first cannon-burst against nineteenth-century theology was really fired by David Hume, the Scottish philosopher (1711–76). Hume's conviction was that all knowledge is ultimately derived from experience. There is no innate information (idea) which precedes our perception of things. We receive sense impressions from which we derive ideas, rather like a faded copy of the original. The mind is simply unable to frame significant concepts about matters that cannot in principle be experienced.

What room does this leave for religion? Not a great deal. Claims made about miracles as proof for confessional belief or about the order of the world and a Divine Cause are improbable at best. Since

115

matter-of-fact experience is our sole source of knowledge, what we *know* is that nature is uniform, regular, and that miracles violate the laws of nature. It can never be *reasonable* to accept miraculous events; other explanations which have their psychological origin in experience would be more sensible. Nor does the utter order of the world necessarily speak of a God beyond the world or of the Christian God, since there is evil as well as order, suffering as well as joy. The Principle who constructed this world need not be perfectly good and surely is not perfectly powerful.

Hume's radical skepticism raised these same problems for any reality that escapes sensible perception. So not only questions like the existence of God, but the immortality of the soul and the freedom of the will were also at stake. Any philosophical, scientific, or religious language that required metaphysical statements, positions that at once met the world of experience but transcended it, were suspect.

Immanuel Kant (1724–1804) set out to answer Hume's objections. Hume woke him from his "dogmatic slumber." In a series of three major works, the *Critiques of Pure Reason, Practical Reason,* and *Teleological Judgement* (and Taste), Kant tried to refound science, morality, religion, and aesthetics on certain grounds. He asked not only *"What* do we know?" but *"How* do we know what we know?" The answer to this second question limits the answers possible for the first.

Kant postulated knowing faculties of sensibility, understanding, and reason. Sensibility perceives the particular data of experience; understanding provides the intellectual schemata or mental equipment (so to speak) by which one may sort out through concepts what one is knowing. These categories are purely formal, that is, they do not give us information, but only provide the proper frames through which we can combine sense data intelligibly. Reason secures the categories of the understanding by means of principles which Kant calls Ideas. These Ideas are the immortality of the soul, the freedom of the will, and the existence of God.

Now if we try to prove the reality of these Ideas through our experience, we fall into complete contradiction. We can just as easily disprove the existence of God as prove it. The same is true for the permanent unity of the psychological subject and the freedom or determinism of the human will. But we know that these formal ideas regulate our whole way of being. We act as if they were the case; indeed, we must live *as though* we were free, a psychological identity—and *as though* God exists.

Kant believed that through his understanding of scientific (or pure) reason, he had provided a symmetry with moral (or practical) reason. Knowing and doing were correlative; but actions were dependent upon the free choices, the risks of belief that something which is the case for me should be that way for all.

Kant viewed aesthetic judgments as a third sort of human option. On the basis of particulars, we judge that something is beautiful not to everyone's taste but that everyone who sees this particular art object will operate with the same imagination and emotive force.

Kant's three critiques tell us something about nineteenth-century theology. In attempting to answer the criticism of David Hume, theologians went through each one of the doors which Kant opened. There were those who disagreed with Kant, trying to locate religious notions in the realm of speculative reason. Some agreed with Kant that religion was primarily an ethical matter, unprovable by rational endeavor. Still others identified religion with the aesthetic and emotional. Catholics opted for all of these in one form or another to understand their faith.

Religion as Moral Reason—Georg Hermes

Georg Hermes (1775–1831) tried to make Catholic theology credible in terms of Kant's notions of scientific certitude. Since God is the most important "object" of religious knowledge, surely we must know for certain that he exists. Redesigning Catholic philosophy, Hermes attempted to show that God could be seen as the absolute Condition for the achievement of any reasonable moral action. If we are going to fulfill our moral obligations, then we must trust in God's authority, which permits us to be certain in our actions. Otherwise, we would be acting in doubt.

Though Hermes realized that his apology for Catholic faith did not look like the old arguments based upon miracles and God's Word, he would not have expected the condemnation of his positions which occurred after his death. Pope Gregory XVI (1831–46) saw only that the act of faith itself was a gift of divine grace, not a reasonable addendum to our achievement of practical affairs.

Religion as Aesthetic Trust in the
History of the Kingdom

The shift in English poetry between Alexander Pope's (1688–1744) heroic couplets and Percy Bysshe Shelley's (1792–1822) lyrics cannot be more obvious. What before had been reason, discipline, and polished manners became expressive passion, eccentric genius, and conventionless freedom. As Samuel Taylor Coleridge (1772–1834) put it: "Deep thinking is attainable only by a man of deep feeling." The poetry, music, and prose of the Romantics—and their theology—were meant to ignite the world. Their inspiration and optimism were inaugurated in the American, then in the early days of the French, Revolutions. As William Blake (1757–1827), the poet and artist, has it in *The Marriage of Heaven and Hell* (1790–93): "Exuberance is Beauty."

German Catholic and Protestant theologians, under the spell of Romanticism, shifted their horizons from the rational and universally demonstrable to the affective and the particular. They embraced both sides of historical studies with passion. The upper blade of the scientific scissors demanded that they think the continuities of past data, searching it for clues to patterns; the lower blade required the recovery of exact facts separated from fable. The first mode of thinking permitted new ways of thinking around or beyond Kant so that the meaning of Christian faith could be reestablished; the second provided accurate data so that theories about faith could never become abstract or unrelated to the actual Tradition.

Johann Sebastian von Drey (1777–1853) and his students boldly undertook to think through the particulars of the Christian Scriptures and Tradition to the meaning of a historical faith. Unlike Hermes's rationalism, Drey's analyses took the Romantics' notion of the universe as an organic developing whole and applied it to Christian revelation. God's creation of the world was his loving disclosure of himself. God's Kingdom is an evolving idea, revealed at the beginning of everything. Social and historical, this idea comes to conscious expression in the Church. The bearer of God's revelation in the present is therefore the growing, changing, social history of humanity, progressively unfolding itself until God gathers the Kingdom into himself. All visible manifestations of ecclesial life are signs, symbols of this generous communication of Love. Faith was not irrational, but a reasonable confidence in God's action in history and society.

Historians like Johann Joseph Ignaz von Döllinger (1799–1890) and Lord Acton (John Emmerich Edward Dahlberg, 1834–1902) believed that the introduction of historical-critical methods could only benefit Catholic self-understanding. Their emphasis upon the tools of research, the hard work of manuscript recovery, the critical analysis which distinguished fact from legend assumed responsibility for the traditions of scholarship begun by the French Benedictines of St. Maur in the seventeenth century and canonized by Leopold von Ranke (1795–1886). To discover what actually happened as opposed to what people thought might have happened requires the skill of a detective and the surgeon's delicate scalpel. Every cherished body of belief which undergoes the suspicions of historical criticism finds the operation painful.

Acton and von Döllinger, however, saw the historical sciences as a "trusty ally." They believed that the actual data of history would bear witness to the truth of Catholic positions. If history did not, then the positions themselves required reconstruction. Acton wrote,

> We are bound to see that the laws of true reasoning and of historical criticism are not tampered with; it is by them only we can know in their reasonableness and integrity the doctrines which have been revealed and developed in the process of history.[2]

Later nineteenth-century controversies required both von Döllinger and Acton to step back from their strenuous matchmaking between contemporary science and the Catholic Tradition. Both continued to believe that the forceful history of truth was the only authentic victory of faith.

Neo-Scholasticism

By midcentury, the strength of the Romantic theological movement had been spent in Catholic circles. Simultaneously, the Middle Ages had been discovered (especially by the English essayists and critics John Ruskin [1819–1900] and William Morris [1834–96]). Here was a premodern society in which thought, action, and religion made a coherent social pattern. Interest in medieval philosophy and theology followed in the attempt to find answers to (what seemed) the rational subjectivism of Kant, the relativism of historically minded theologians, and the political criticism of progressives.

The Jesuits were in the forefront of this recovery of the past with their restoration (1814) after political suppression in 1773. Men like Joseph Kleutgen (1811–83) used political power and the Society's organs of communication (the Roman College, now the Gregorianum, and the journal *Civiltà Cattolica*) to foster the replacement of all modern systems of philosophy or theology with the study of Thomas Aquinas.

Kleutgen's opposition to newer theologies turned on the belief that contemporaries confused or intermixed the act of faith and the role of reason; the action of God's grace and independent, though subordinate, value of nature; and the interdependent coprinciples of soul and body. Theologies such as Drey's which believed that the movement of history was at once God's action *and* human choice were immediately suspect, though his particular opinions were never condemned. The rationalism of Hermes, however, proved to be a confused mixture of faith and reason. Reason and faith, nature and grace, body and soul were not opposed to each other; but in each case, the second contrary was only a helpmate to supernatural values.

Kleutgen's recovery of the Aristotelian bases for Aquinas's theories of knowlege (epistemology) permitted him to develop a knowing subject who was capable of metaphysical arguments for the existence of God *and* a sure knowledge of ethical judgments based upon the natural law. Contemporary thinkers had either rejected Divine Presence on the basis of sense (empiricism, e.g., Hume) or immanentized Divine Presence in a pantheist subject (idealism). An authentic Aquinas would permit not only a true theory of knowledge (*how* we know), but also a metaphysics (*what* we know), guaranteeing a society of secure moral roles.

Kleutgen's presentations were overwhelmingly successful. Although we know now that his understanding of Aquinas was rather defective, nonetheless, he had given Thomism an intellectual respectability it had probably never had before. He had shown that spirituality, practice, and truth were a religious unity which should not be divided in the contemporary world. His positions would be emended, contradicted, and surpassed; but he provided the base for the rich reinterpretations of Aquinas by Étienne Gilson (1884–1978), Jacques Maritain (1882–1973), and Joseph Maréchal (1878–1944) as well as the contemporary analyses of Karl Rahner (b. 1904) and Bernard Lonergan (b. 1904). The future was in the seeds of the past.

POPE PIUS IX—THE PAPAL STATES AND VATICAN COUNCILS

Pope Pius IX (1792–1878) began his pontificate in 1846 as a reformer in the lands under his civil jurisdiction. He granted amnesties, proposed economic reforms and social changes which widened electoral representation. He was determined to strengthen the dilapidated state bequeathed to him by Pope Gregory XVI (1831–46) or the puppet state which Napoleon I (1769–1821) had wrested from Pius VII (1800–1823). With this history, it is not surprising that the existence of the Papal States seemed, even to some liberal Catholics, an essential instrument for the independence of the head of the Catholic Church.

Over the period of a year, Pius granted more and more authority to democratic bodies subordinate to the papacy until, in 1848, he granted a new constitution making himself, in effect, a limited ruling monarch. In April, however, he refused to allow papal troops to join the Catholic King of Piedmont-Sardinia in a war against Catholic Austria; and shortly thereafter terrorists assassinated his prime minister in Parliament. Pius fled to Naples in disguise, returning only when French troops occupied Rome. This military security remained in the city from 1849 until 1870, when their removal occasioned the takeover of the Papal States by the forces of Italian unification. Pius remained intransigently opposed to any compromise with modern democratic ideals.

During the last two decades of his pontificate, Pius turned to "spiritual" affairs where his strong conserving voice was not always reactionary. He erected new dioceses and restored the episcopal hierarchies to England (1850) and Holland (1853). But his two

121

major successes were the proclamation of the doctrine of the immaculate conception of the Virgin Mary (1854) and the decrees of the First Vatican Council (1869–70).

In the proclamation of 1854, centuries-old devotion to the Mother of Jesus, which had grown largely without any official ecclesiastical discussion since the Council of Ephesus (431), received institutional approbation, support, and correction. Pius, encouraged by the bishops whom he had consulted and by Catholic piety, declared Mary's immaculate conception a dogma, that is, an official belief of the community. The theological meaning of the dogma was stated clearly. Mary, because of her office and role as the Mother of Jesus, was conceived without the sin (Original Sin) which is the heritage of all human beings. This did not mean that Mary had been raised to the level of Redeemer; but that as the Mother of the Redeemer, she shared beforehand in the grace of his life and work. Her own conception and birth were quite normal; the statement was a religious, not a biological, one—that Mary is the first of the redeemed; that indeed, if she is not the ultimately faithful disciple, pondering all things in her heart, not one of us can be.

The culminating accomplishment of Pius's reforming conservatism is far more important for the Catholic world—the first general council of the Church since Trent (1545–63). Its dogmatic constitution *Dei Filius* (*Son of God*) recalled Catholics to their scholastic heritage, best described as a middle course between the theological temptations of fideism (faith alone without, or in opposition to, the use of human reason) and rationalism (reason alone without faith). The council fathers reminded their contemporaries that, at least since the time of Anselm of Canterbury (1034–1109), the Catholic ideal for theology must include both faith and reason.

Reason provides *some* understanding of the mysteries of faith, partially from analogues in the natural world, partially from comparison with other beliefs of the community. Catholics must continue to be "pilgrims in this mortal life, not yet with God; 'for we walk by faith and not by sight'" (2 Cor. 5:7, NAB). Art and science, with their own methods and principles, contribute to this life of faith; and authentic art or science can never really be in opposition to faith.

The most controversial conservative document of the Council,

122

however, is that concerning the infallibility of the pope in matters of faith and morals. There were, of course, political undertones to the decree. Pius IX had centered loyalty to the Church more and more upon allegiance to the papacy; political events demanded it, according to his mind. Nor was it possible for him or his opponents to see a distinction between his role as sovereign of civil territory and servant-head of the Church. Civil war against the pope was destruction of his spiritual authority.

The internal dissension between liberals and conservatives in the Church repeated itself in their attitudes toward the papacy. Some, usually called the Ultramontanes, claimed extravagant power for the papal office. Strong support of the papacy in France went along with strong opposition to civil control of the Church. There was a bizarre coherence between thinking of Pius IX as "the most enlightened sovereign of the age" (as one London newspaper phrased it) and the "vice-God of humanity" (as a French bishop remarked). One Italian Ultramontanist described it this way: "When the Pope thinks, it is God who is thinking in him."[3]

These extravagances, seemingly so blasphemous now, were not isolated. Opponents before and during the Council felt that it was utterly inopportune, though not perhaps inaccurate, to describe the pope as infallible. They generally feared the particular sort of infallibility which might be defined.

The Council, however, was not a rubber stamp for the thoughts of Pius IX. It is now clear that there was quite adequate time for nuanced discussion and moderate revision of the decree on the Church and infallibility which ultimately emerged from the Council halls.

The doctrine of infallibility reasserts the belief that God will not let the Church be led into major errors on basic questions of faith and morality. As a result, solemn pronouncements upon urgent matters of faith and morals by a pope, when he speaks not as an individual but for and to the universal Church, cannot be erroneous. It is thus the charism (or spiritual gift) and power of teaching that is protected in this dogmatic statement of the council. However, not all papal teaching is protected, only the teaching on issues of consequence in faith or morals.

Vatican Council I represents a high point of traditional Catholi-

123

cism in the nineteenth century. The development of more far-reaching Catholic reforms lay ahead, for the prime issue continued to be the separation of most Catholics from the wider culture of political democracy and contemporary science. Pius himself seems to have understood that an era was passing. Shortly before his death, he is reported to have said:

> I hope my successor will be as much attached to the Church as I have been and will have as keen a desire to do good: beyond that, I can see that everything has changed; my system and my policies have had their day, but I am too old to change my course; that will be the task of my successor.[4]

THE PROPHETS OF THE FUTURE

Change came swiftly. European Catholicism saw a shift to the forces of liberalism at the highest level. Upon the death of Pius IX in 1878, Cardinal Gioacchino Vicenzo Pecci (1810–1903), formerly a student of Jesuit Neo-Scholasticism and papal diplomat to Brussels, London, Paris, and Cologne, was elected as Leo XIII. Making use of the enormous prestige gained in the Catholic Church by the emphasis upon the role of the pope, Leo wrote significant letters, encyclicals, outlining creative resolutions to the interchange between Church and world (*Immortale Dei*, 1885) and describing the freedom of citizens in republics (*Libertas Praestantissimum*, 1888) and in Christian democracies (*Graves in Communi*, 1901). He established the return to the authentic texts of Thomas Aquinas as the proper educational tool for theological students (*Aeterni Patris*, 1889) and encouraged the critical study of the Bible (*Providentissimus Deus*, 1893). He opened the Vatican archives to historical research (1883) and established a Biblical Commission (1902) to deal with questions of interpretation by a committee of scholarly peers. As Leo stated: "The first law of history is to dare not to lie; the second is not to fear to speak the truth—and to leave no room for prejudice." Probably his most renowned encyclical, however, is *Rerum Novarum* (1891), which comments on the social, religious, and political value of labor, property, government, and industrial society. This letter established a program of social reform which has been reiterated to the present by continuing papal support.

Just as one prophet of future Catholic life was an Italian pope, the other was an English cardinal, a convert from the Church of England. John Henry Newman (1801–90) reflects the creative stature and shifting energies of nineteenth-century Catholicism perhaps better than any other. As he himself put it: "To be human is to change; to be perfect is to change often."

Newman's own life made this ideal concrete. As an Anglican clergyman, he quickened the reforming tempo of the Church of England through the Oxford Movement (1833–45). As a Roman Catholic priest, he helped, by his own historical research, to promote a needed awareness of the biblical and patristic origins of the Catholic Tradition. As an Englishman, he brought the British empirical, scientific, and historical traditions into contact with continental Catholicism. As a thinker and believer, he made it clear that he could not and would not leave aside anything that was fundamentally human in his presentation of faith. And finally, as one of the foremost prose writers in his century, Newman created a style which could communicate to all readers the meaning of a life spent in search of religious values.

In his *Essay on the Development of Doctrine* (1845), Newman outlined how history and critical historical research itself can be aids to the understanding of changing beliefs. As his intellectual interpretation for becoming a Catholic, the *Essay* described how the Church had changed throughout the past and how believers can only anticipate that it will continue to do so in the present and the future.

The Newman one remembers most winningly is the quiet, stringently honest, straightforward man whose autobiography, *Apologia pro Vita Sua* (1864), registers all the thoughtful tensions and affective paradoxes, the religious heights of conversion and the depressive depths of sin that an individual can undergo in the quest to be both modern and Catholic. In his *Essay in Aid of a Grammar of Assent* (1870), Newman's mature reflections on the relation between faith and reason provide an analysis not of concepts nor of abstract truths, but of the act of faith itself. What are we doing when we believe? Is it a contemporary possibility?

Newman comprised in his life and understanding of that faithful life the three major concerns that had occupied most of nineteenth-century Catholicism: *who* the believer is (subjectivity); *how* the believer comes to faith (history); and *why* the believer should trust the Christian faith as socially, philosophically, and politically credible (reason). Newman's original contributions to these questions of theology, culture, philosophy, and history were not always appreciated by Catholics in the nineteenth century. Somewhat suspicious of his arguments, they could not have guessed that in 1879, Leo XIII would grant Newman the cardinalate. There is here no finer symbol of Newman's achievements as an individual believer or of the success of the progressive forces whose triumph he represented in the Catholic Church.

HEARING THE STRAINS OF FUTURE HARMONIES

The nineteenth-century Catholic experience ended in quite another key than it began. From Napoleon's hegemony over Pius VII to Leo XIII's invitation to the modern world is a shift in form. The contrasts and dissonances with the powerful position of papal authority transformed themselves into a chorus of praise with conservative dissidents. The century's Catholic history seems to the uninitiated or uninterested much like a later symphony of Anton Bruckner (1824–96)—lengthy, formless swells of passion, sharply broken by reasonable melodies lasting but a moment, alternately loud, then soft, ending rather then concluding.

But the century's Catholic identity is merely complex. The polarizations at its beginning—either the modern world or the Church; either critical history or the Bible; either democratic freedom or papal authority; either the philosophy of the human subject or objective beliefs—did find their positive resolution in prophetic figures such as the early Lamennais, von Döllinger, Acton, and Newman—and curiously enough in Neo-Scholastics like Kleutgen and popes like Leo XIII. It is in those dramatic figures, and many others whom we have not named, who were willing to risk scientific history in their faith and to embody action based upon history, science, and faith, that a vision of a Catholic Church in the twentieth century was achieved.

NOTES

1. Igor Stravinsky, *Poetics of Music,* trans. Arthur Knodel and Ingolf Dahl (Cambridge, Mass.: Harvard University Press, 1979), 33–42.
2. Lord Acton, *Essays on Church and State,* ed. Douglas Woodruff (New York: Crowell, 1968), 273.
3. See Cuthbert Butler, *The Vatican Council, 1869–70,* ed. Christopher Butler (Westminster, Md.: Newman, 1962), 44–62.
4. Alec R. Vidler, *The Church in an Age of Revolution: 1789 to the Present Day* (Baltimore: Penguin Books, 1968), 153.

FURTHER RELATED MATERIAL

Stephen Neill's, *The Interpretation of the New Testament 1861–1961* (New York and London: Oxford University Press, 1966) chronicles nineteenth- and twentieth-century biblical developments affecting theology. Paul Tillich (*Perspectives on 19th and 20th Century Protestant Theology*, ed. K. Braaten [New York: Harper & Row, 1967]) and Karl Barth (*Protestant Theology in the Nineteenth Century* [Valley Forge, Pa.: Judson, 1973]) offer contrasting Protestant understandings of the development of the period. Catholic theology of the period is excellently presented in Gerald McCool, *Catholic Theology in the Nineteenth Century: The Quest for a Unitary Method* (New York: Seabury Press, 1977). The political and religious grid is admirably described in E. E. Y. Hales, *Pio Nono: A Study of European Politics and Religion in the Nineteenth Century* (Garden City, N.Y.: Doubleday & Co., 1962), while Cuthbert Butler, *The Vatican Council, 1869–70,* ed. Christopher Butler (Westminster, Md.: Newman, 1962) offers a still helpful view of the previous Vatican Council. Mark Schoof's *A Survey of Catholic Theology, 1800–1970,* trans. N. D. Smith (New York: Paulist, 1970), while sometimes spotty and episodic, nonetheless describes the major figures. A. R. Vidler's *The Church in an Age of Revolution: 1789 to the Present Day* (Baltimore: Penguin Books, 1968) overviews the whole. An intellectual vision of the entire period is best presented with added bibliography and helpful questions in James C. Livingston, *Modern Christian Thought from the Enlightenment to Vatican II* (New York: Macmillan Co., 1971).

10

THE CREATORS OF
TWENTIETH-CENTURY CATHOLICISM (I)
Europe: Prophets from the Past,
Pastors for the Future

> It is done.
> Once again the Fire has penetrated the earth.
> Not with the sudden crash of thunderbolt,
> Riving the mountain tops:
> Does the Master break down doors to enter his own home?
> Without earthquake, or thunderclap:
> The flame has lit up the whole world from within.
>   Pierre Teilhard de Chardin (1881–1955),
>   from *Hymn of the Universe*

Our world is made of images—moving pictures, video recordings, photographic reprints. We fix on film certain ways of seeing, knowing something or someone. We still the mobile present into a past we can detach from a book, an album, and handle or repeat it—sometimes with loving care, sometimes with desire, occasionally with fear and hatred. Pictures, as Susan Sontag has noted, have become a defense against our anxieties about the transience of things and friends, a tool to establish control.[1] If we have in our possession birthday pictures of our children for the first fifteen years, if we have family Christmas ensembles imprinted on paper, then we control the change in our children and the divisions in our families in the present. We can look in on a time in which we once were "all together."

If our overview of the history of Catholicism—of its prophets, apocalyptic visionaries, and proponents of Tradition—is seen as merely a lengthy group portrait of our occasionally inept, sometimes saintly, even brilliant ancestors, then we have failed. For the modern meaning of Catholicism must be a *cumulative* presence of questions, heroes and heroines, texts and places which continue to surprise the Church with its active memory.

The contemporary shape of the Church attempts to come to terms with its own universality, its own catholic nature. If in the post-Reformation period the Church saw itself providing a uniform cultural alternative to the confusions, disagreements, and anger of early modern societies, it now recognizes that universality will require not an abstract unique culture, but a strong network of interlocking cultural expressions of Christian spirituality, action, and beliefs. It is a vocation to the concrete Catholic incarnation of the Gospel, whatever the cost to itself.

Thus there remain those who continuously propose the Tradition, and their extraordinary gift to the future was the Second Vatican Council (1962–65). There are the prophets who constantly call the Church to social justice, political freedom for the oppressed, food for the hungry, and they come regularly from those countries where former colonial powers were once exploitive. Then there are the visionaries—those who can see only God's future in a world dominated by the threat of nuclear war, a population explosion with its consequent crises of food, resources, and international terrorism.

In the three chapters that conclude our survey of Catholic identity, we will discuss these people, places, and things in a sequence that begins in Europe where the Tradition recently has been so brightly refurbished and continues in the United States where the principle of religious freedom has been upheld. We will finish our journey in the world of Latin America, Asia, and Africa, where the future dreams of criticism and hope seem to lie. But our vision of the Catholic future begins in recovery of the Catholic past.

A QUESTION OF THE PAST: REACTIONS AND RECOVERY OF OPINIONS

The Crisis of Modernity

When Pius X (1835–1914) was elected in 1903, this utterly pious man (later declared a saint [1954]) announced that in contrast to the politically and educationally progressive initiatives of his predecessor Leo XIII, he would "restore all things in Christ" (Eph. 1:10). His program for restoration included the growing involvement of lay Catholics in the missionary life of the Church, a new codification of Canon Law (the first since the Middle Ages), reforms of the prayer life and Eucharist of the Church—and the annihilation of Modernism.

130

Most scholars now agree that Modernism, defined by Pius's papal letters *Pascendi* and *Lamentabili* (1907) as a "synthesis of all heresies," was less a movement than a loose combination of individuals faced with the problems of modernity in the Catholic Church. They were concerned about the same range of questions as their "liberal" forebears (such as De Lamennais): the acceptance of historical-critical method in biblical research, the rigidity of the reigning scholasticisms, growing papal authoritarianism, and the Church's affiliation with repressive political regimes. But they combined these issues with a recognition that the religious experience of Christianity, precisely as *religious,* transcended all narratives, symbols, interpretations, institutions, and systems.

Even though critics of papal policy think the decrees were an extremely skillful articulation of the logical implications of contemporary ideas, most would agree that no matter how clever the construction, the reaction was hasty, regrettably defensive, and even panic-stricken. The primary error of Modernism, according to its opponents, was its reduction of religious truth to personal religious experience. Sacraments, dogmas, and hierarchy were dispensable expressions judged by the private needs of the individual. The encyclical saw the movement as a contemporary form of Docetism, an ancient heresy in which Christ did not so much *become* human with all its limitations as cloak his divinity in a discardable humanity.

Though upon occasion some Modernists were somewhat devious in the propagation of their ideas (through the use of pseudonyms), the suspicious reactions created as much of a crisis as the ideas themselves. A concerted effort was made in dioceses throughout the world to hunt out avant-garde thinkers, requiring candidates for ordination, seminary professors, and theologians to take an anti-Modernist oath. Schools of theology fostered stricter behavior and more rigid teaching called Integrism, which always harshly and loudly proclaimed its loyalty to the past. This sometimes hysterically reactionary element, with its pattern of spies and informers, remains a raw nerve in Catholic life to the present day.

Pius X sensed, rather than thought, that there must be a halt to scholarship before the Church was captured in images in which it could no longer recognize its continuity with its own identity. For the Modernists, the crisis was one of methods: of the Church's ability to adapt creatively to a new situation. What is the truth of the situation?

What did Modernists teach? We must look briefly at three individuals: Alfred Loisy (1857–1940), a French Scripture scholar; George Tyrell (1861–1909), a Jesuit theologian and essayist; and Friedrich von Hügel (1852–1925), layman, philosopher of religion, and theologian. The first two were excommunicated from the Church; von Hügel, though suspect, escaped censure.

Alfred Loisy—Biblical Critic

Loisy believed that his mission was to reconcile contemporary critical scholarship of the Bible with the essence of Catholicism. As a professor in Paris, he lectured against the factual character of the early chapters of Genesis. Dismissed from his professorship (1893), he wrote a response to Adolf von Harnack's (1851–1930) *The Essence of Christianity* (1900), which he saw as a "liberal" misreading of the New Testament. In his *The Gospel and the Church* Loisy argued that the most primitive Jesus-texts were the proclamations of the imminence of the kingdom, not the Fatherhood of God, the infinite value of the individual soul, and an ideal of ethical living, as von Harnack thought. This eschatological kingdom *had to give way* to the doctrinal institutionalizations of the Church. Jesus announced the kingdom; it was the Church that arrived.

This biblical critic thought of his position as an eminently pastoral defense of the Tradition through which the New Testament was written. Development was essential to the very existence of a Catholic community. Ecclesiastical formulas are not the object of faith, since only God himself, Christ, and his work can guide the contemporary Church.

Loisy's somewhat left-handed support for Catholic identity was received with suspicion. His assumptions that the Gospels were not historical biographies of Jesus; that they were only testimonies of belief by early communities; that Jesus' own consciousness of his mission was limited, even erroneous; and that doctrines are a change in the substance of the Tradition did not fit the prevailing understandings of Catholic experience.

George Tyrell—Mystical Doctrine

During George Tyrell's early years as a convert to Catholicism, he became an ardent disciple of Thomas Aquinas; but late in the century

132

he came into contact with other philosophies. The conflict this produced caused him to reject all authoritarian forms of doctrine— but not to disavow Catholicism. The Modernist, unlike the liberal, adheres to both modernity and Tradition. "By the modernist, I mean a churchman, of any sort, who believes in the possibility of a synthesis between the essential truth of his religion and the essential truth of modernity."[2]

Tyrell, like Loisy, had a certain mystical temperament which believed that the practical return of the heart's love to God was more important than any theoretic or institutional formulation. Faith in the continuity of spiritual revelation precedes parables and facts. Institutions and constructs are symbols of the essentially transcendent religious ideal. When we read his remarks about the Church, we cannot help but think of later words by Vatican Council II. Tyrell states that Christ

> lives in the Church, not metaphorically but actually. He finds a growing medium of self-utterance, ever complementing and correcting that of His mortal individuality. . . . The Church is not merely a society or school, but a mystery and sacrament; like the humanity of Christ of which it is an extension.[3]

Friedrich von Hügel—Spiritual Teacher

Baron von Hügel was a philosopher of religion, a director of troubled souls, and an authority on mysticism with or without his Modernist connections. Born in Florence, educated in Europe, settling near London, he became the intellectual switchboard for the Modernist conversation. His distrust of Scholasticism was as profound as Tyrell's; he found it incapable of including the historical, the experiential, and the critical. His convictions concerning the use of biblical scholarship were just as severe as Loisy's. Yet he neither left the Church nor did the Church leave him. Why?

Von Hügel was absolutely convinced of the cognitive, even strictly metaphysical, element in every religious experience. He lamented the fact that his friends were non- or antiphilosophical. Doctrine was an integral moment of all experience, especially religious experience. Secondly, von Hügel was deeply attached to the institutional Church. The Catholic Church embodied for him the spiritual experience of humanity and his personal piety depended upon it. Finally, von Hügel was a diplomat, a master of European languages, whose ability and will to mediate among opposing parties no doubt reflected a certain mental ability which permitted his seeing many sides of an issue simultaneously.

Though von Hügel considered the papal decrees of 1907 deeply unjust, he also understood, particularly later in life, how unsatisfactory some of his friends' philosophical and ecclesial positions were. For him, Christianity was three interlocking, overlapping spheres: the mystical, the intellectual, *and* the institutional. None could be ignored except at the risk of losing Catholic identity.

The Modernists identified the problem facing the Catholic Church at the turn of the century as one of culture rather than of faith. It is also clear now that none of the participants had an adequate set of methods (philological, interpretive, historical, or metaphysical) to deal constructively with the problems they had isolated. Although their attempts to update Catholicism through scientific tools were urgently required, they often ignored authentic institutional elements of the past in their understanding of the present.

Painful as the Modernists' views were to the "official" Church, the conflict itself can be viewed historically as the final sour breath of nineteenth-century reactionary attitudes. Yet the consternation at the excesses of Modernists created an impasse in Catholic life, heightening the temptation to forget the claims modernity has on faith.

A Return to the Sources

Fortunately the heedless neglect of modernity, fostered by the squinting response of the papal office to Modernism, did not destroy the intellectual and religious quest of Catholic thinkers. From the end of the nineteenth century, partially due to the fear created by Integrist suspicions, intellectuals began gathering the evidence of the past which would develop in midcentury into a full reconstruction of Catholic life.

The *liturgical revival,* begun by Abbot Prosper Guéranger (1805–75) at the Abbey of Solesmes as a somewhat nostalgic return to medieval piety and music, rapidly gained intellectual and institutional weight through Pope Pius X's support. A largely monastic and Benedictine development under Lambert Beauduin (1873–1960), of

Mont César in Belgium, and Pius Parsch (1884–1954), an Austrian Augustinian canon, it stressed lay participation in worship and encouraged less-perfunctory performance of ritual. People joined in the Eucharist through dialogue and read translations of the liturgical texts while the priest prayed in Latin. Critical and historical studies by Louis Duchesne (1843–1922) and Fernand Cabrol (1855–1937) gave scholarly support to the movement of piety and reform.

The *biblical revival* introduced historical-critical and philological methods into the interpretation of the Christian Scriptures. Marie-Joseph Lagrange (1855–1938) founded the École Pratique d'Études Bibliques in Jerusalem (1890), writing commentaries on both Jewish and Christian Scriptures that rapidly became standard. In 1902, when Leo XIII established the Biblical Commission to promote and supervise biblical studies, Lagrange was made a member.

The *patristic revival* picked up the standard of the Maurists, Cardinal Newman, and Ignaz von Döllinger. It cataloged sources, established critical editions of texts, translated into vernaculars, distinguished legendary from factual narrative, and produced serious biographies. By individuals like F. X. Funk (1840–1907) at Tübingen, Heinrich Dénifle (1844–1905) of the Vatican Archives, Duchesne and his student Pierre Batiffol (1861–1928), Ludwig von Pastor (1854–1928), whose history of the popes became a critical norm, and Charles Joseph Héfèle (1809–93), whose *History of the Councils* (1855–90) with its twentieth-century additions (1907–38) by Henri Leclerq (1869–1945) provided an accurate record of doctrinal change, the data of the Catholic Tradition were established with scientific rigor.

Nor did *philosophical studies* forget a return to their sources. Leo XIII's and Pius X's emphasis on Thomas Aquinas as the most important theologian entailed a new edition of his works and the creative recovery of Aquinas's thought in individuals like Joseph Maréchal (1878–1944), Jacques Maritain (1882–1973), Pierre Rousselot (1878–1915), and Étienne Gilson (1884–1978). The early works of the three most important Catholic systematic theologians of the mid–twentieth century were reinterpretations of Aquinas on epistemology and metaphysics (Karl Rahner [b. 1904]); on grace and human freedom (Bernard Lonergan [b. 1904]) and on sacrament (Edward Schillebeeckx [b. 1914]). Recent work has also rethought the place of other scholastics (for example, Bonaventure and Duns Scotus).

Two major nonscholastic philosophers have influenced twentieth-century theology as well. Through the concrete analysis by Maurice Blondel (1861–1949) of the human will and its inability to be entirely satisfied by particulars, Catholic theologians have been able to emphasize the experiential components of religious knowledge. In Gabriel Marcel (1889–1973), Catholics found a philosophy of existential and interpersonal encounter which validated the noncognitive, though not irrational, aspects of Christian life. These philosophers, by their emphasis on both metaphysical and existential aspects of existence, have proven helpful in going beyond the Modernist tendency to make theologians choose between being or person; philosophy or experience.

The easiest way to understand the basic thrust of this multidimensional movement of change after the Modernist crisis is to hear the French word that symbolizes the whole period from 1920 to 1960—*ressourcement*. The basic meaning of the word is *return*, but as a widespread recalling of the sources of Catholicism. Recalling becomes rehearing the original message; and Catholic *ressourcement* invoked critical investigation and reassessment of the present in the light of the past.

In these various scholarly revivals, Catholics joined their Protestant colleagues in the scientific study of the original documents of their beliefs. Not only did this collaboration provide the initial steps toward the healing of confessional differences, but it established a common thirst for authentic Christian service to the world. Analyses still produce disagreements, but rarely upon confessional loyalties. It has permitted forms of common worship which respect the present institutional disunity, but grant it no angry permanence. Catholics and Protestants have begun to remember a common Tradition.

THE EXISTENTIAL CRISIS—
DEPRESSION AND WORLD WARS

The scholarly revivals, the ecumenical movement, and the encounter with philosophical theories all occurred during two brutal, devastating wars which framed a financially enervating depression. During such periods in an international community, one has the preservers and the risk-takers; those who would prefer to avoid conflict as well as those who would provoke it for the sake of polarizing the evangelical or demonic values involved. The official, institutional Church took both positions.

The underlying goal of every pope was to remain sufficiently neutral in political conflicts so that the charitable, social, educational, and religious endeavors of the Church might continue. Whether it was Benedict XV's (1914–22) neutrality and negotiations for peace, or Pius XI's (1922–39) concordats and treaties with Soviet, German, and Italian nationalist states, the practice of diplomacy with governments was not meant as approval, but as a political enablement for pastoral care. In the case of the Lateran Treaty (1929) with Benito Mussolini's (1883–1945) government, Pius XI wanted neither a simple identification with fascist policies and repression, nor utter antagonism toward governmental attempts at social and economic stabilization.

Yet when the German bishops asked for a papal encyclical on the problems of their Church, Pius responded with a vigorous condemnation of National Socialism (*Mit brennender Sorge,* 1937). No one may put state, government, national religion, or blood-race in the place of God. Shortly before he died, the pope repeated his summons to Catholics by recalling that in the Eucharistic Prayer we call on Abraham as the patriarch and forefather of all. "It is impossible for a Christian to take part in anti-Semitism. It is inadmissible. Through Christ and in Christ we are the spiritual progeny of Abraham. Spiritually, we are all Semites."[4]

The complexity of ecclesiastical response to totalitarian governments during the Second World War (1939–45) reflected the public diplomatic fears and the private charity of Pius XII (1939–58). As a former official representative in Berlin, he had protested bitterly (in some forty notes) on behalf of the papacy against Nazi persecution of Church and peoples. As pope, however, his careful, scholarly use of the international media (especially Vatican radio) proved too general, too abstractly principled to anti-German forces. Pius gave Vatican City passports to refugees, hostages, and Jewish detainees, housing them in extraterritorial Vatican buildings all during the war; but his lack of direct confrontation with Nazism contrasted too distinctly with the growing acerbic anger of Pius XI.

Like all diplomats, Pius XII seemed to believe that reasonable solutions were always possible. That such approaches were sufficient in the case of specific atrocities, like the deportation and holocaust of European Jews, is not only questionable but impossible. During the war, various Jewish groups thanked the pope for his interventions in the preservation of some four hundred thousand Jews from certain death. Yet in this era of precisely institutional responses, was that enough to claim loyalty to a Tradition engendered by Jesus of Nazareth?

Pius left the heroism of the institution to the corporate responsibility of national bishops and individual martyrs. And there were martyrs at all levels, individuals like Edith Stein (1891–1942), a Carmeline nun, philosopher, teacher, and writer, who was removed from her Dutch refuge to Auschwitz where she died in the gas chambers; or Maximilian Kolbe (1894–1941), a Polish Franciscan, who offered to replace a young prisoner who had a family. He died of starvation at Auschwitz. Even though Pius XII feared reprisals against Catholics in Germany and in occupied Europe, bishops like Michael von Faulhaber (1869–1952) of Munich and Clemens A. von Galen (1878–1946) of Münster publicly condemned euthanasia, concentration camps, imprisonment without trial, and confiscation of property. Priests like Rupert Mayer (1876–1945) maintained that a German Catholic could never be a National Socialist, spoke out, and received imprisonment as a response. Yet in the end, nothing is enough to remove the common responsibility of the Churches and Western Allies in not speaking earlier, with more forcefulness, and with greater effectiveness. We may not justify ourselves in the face of sin.

THE RISE OF A PROPHET—POPE JOHN XXIII

In the postwar years, Catholics needed a prophetic and dramatic figure, a new apostle who could communicate the progressive advancements of Church life in the face of the denials of war, depression, and death. One of the most amazing "accidents" of Catholic history occurred in the appearance of a prophet who was also pope, an authority who was servant.

Pope John XXIII (1958–63) was astounding by any standard. The style of Pius XII's government had been authoritarian and triumphal; in his later years, his considerable intellectual abilities waned and his native conserving *Romanità* could see no further than the crises of his early papacy. By contrast, John XXIII was Francis of Assisi raised to the role of Peter in the Church. His pontificate was brief; but when he died, the entire self-understanding of most Catholics had changed.

The impact of this pope was not so much that of intellect, though he had been a shrewd diplomat, nor of program, but of person. He appeared as a pastor and common father to all peoples of the world. His final encyclical, *Pacem in Terris* (*Peace on Earth*, 1963), was addressed to all men and women of good will. When he called together the few cardinals present in Rome for a meeting in January 1959, few realized how momentous his papacy would be. His agenda announced a few reforms and the calling of an ecumenical council. He saw its purpose as threefold: to link the bishops of the world to the pastoral responsibilities of the Bishop of Rome, to begin a reform or *aggiornamento* (Italian for "updating") of the Church itself, and to promote Christian unity. Pope John's personal attitudes were so outgoing that he could no longer maintain the policy of earlier Catholic withdrawal from contemporary intellectual and political life. Cardinal Montini, then archbishop of Milan and later pope as Paul VI (1963–78), remarked that it would be "the greatest Council the Church has ever held in the whole of the twenty centuries of its history. . . . Before our eyes, history is opening up enormous prospects for centuries to come."[5]

A NEW PENTECOST—
THE SECOND VATICAN COUNCIL (1962–65)

When the Council opened with a membership of approximately twenty-five hundred bishops and representatives of other Christian churches, the pope described the apocalyptic and condemnatory policy he hoped the fathers would repudiate. Those "prophets of doom" who saw in society only ruinous calamities should discover the "mysterious designs of divine Providence." Although the rejection of the old style of institutional distance to the world happened slowly, the Council did attempt to reshape the Church's pastoral role in an expanding culture. The declarations of the Council directed themselves to the reordering of Catholic institutional life, the relation of the Church to other Christians and nonbelievers, and to the world as a whole.

Inner Life: Worship and Collegiality

Through documents on worship, revelation, and the Church, the Council hoped to confirm the newly developing expressions of Catholic self-awareness. The *Constitution on the Sacred Liturgy* (1963) called for a simpler, more biblical worship which would engage the participation of the entire congregation. This was most clearly signaled in the return to the vernacular languages of believers, the removal of privatized prayers and merely ornamental gestures. It promoted the possibility of an utterly international style of indigenous liturgical evolution, reversing the uniformity which had so characterized the reforms dependent upon the Council of Trent.

Changes in worship were paralleled by a growing understanding of the Church itself. The *Dogmatic Constitution on the Church* (1964) and the *Decree on the Bishop's Pastoral Office in the Church* (1965), together with those on lay activity and priesthood, identified the Church as collegial (i.e., with an authority held in common, like a college). The Church has concentric circles of shared (or co-) responsibility among all members, with each member taking responsibility in his or her own way.

This notion of authority is strikingly different from that of a previous era in which the "common laity" were at the base of a pyramidal, layered communication that saw clergy (priests and bishops, then the pope) at the hierarchical apex. An ecclesial authority whose self-understanding had been largely *stratified,* that is, settled in ever higher and higher rungs of responsibility, was now describing itself as *differentiated* or dependent upon the differing competencies of the roles held in the community. The bishops saw themselves as completing the work begun at Vatican Council I when it defined the infallibility of the papal office. All authority in the episcopal office originates in Christ's death and resurrection as the service of redemption. Each bishop holds his authority directly from Christ's office, but in relationship to all others and to the primacy of the Bishop of Rome.

This technical, theological emphasis upon collegial responsibility has had important practical effects in Catholic communities. It has fostered the sharing of tasks and duties in national conferences of bishops; associations and senates of priests; evangelical, diocesan, and pastoral councils of laymen and women; and the local lay consultants called parish councils. The conciliar constitution led to a major decentralization of official authority and an increasing democratization of the Church (also with its consequent bureaucratization as well) on both the international and local levels.

The Council's ability to resee Catholicism in biblical and patristic images—the people of God, the Church as mystery, as sacrament ("a sign and instrument of communion with God and unity among all"), "holy, yet in need of purification," a prophetic and eschatological community—could not have been accomplished if it had not listened again to revelation itself (*Word of God,* 1965). The decree supported biblical scholarship, promoted the teaching of Scripture, and described revelation itself as God's disclosure of his own love, available in the faithful preaching of the prophets and apostles, crystallized in the Scriptures and Tradition which continue to interpret them.

Relations with the Future

In its four autumn sessions, however, the Council not only looked at reforms within the Church, but through its use of Protestant "observers" found ways to describe the common life of believers in the larger world. In the *Constitution on the Church* (1964) and the *Decree on Ecumenism* (1964), diatribe and the parochialism of withdrawal were decisively rejected for a fresh spirit of collaborative respect.

This new ecumenism was especially true for Catholics in relationship to their Jewish brothers and sisters. One of the darkest stains on the records of our Christian past has been the anti-Semitism which expressed conscious and unconscious motivations through harassment, persecution, and programs of racial destruction. The conciliar fathers made a first, if halting, attempt to atone for previous Christian sins of omission and commission by removing from Jews, as a people and as individuals, the charge of deicide (i.e., the killing of God). Efforts were made, though they were not wholly successful due to the opposition of Middle-Eastern Christians, to offer support for the national, political existence of Israel (established in 1948). "Spiritually, we are all Semites," as Pius XI had reminded us.

In two further documents, the *Declaration on Religious Freedom* (1965) and the *Pastoral Constitution on the Church in the Modern World* (1965), the Church declared its openness to the true values of contemporary modernity. Largely inspired by the writings of the United States Jesuit John Courtney Murray (1904–67), the *Declaration* affirmed the value of religious freedom for all people in all nations. The Church was not releasing individuals from their responsibility to be religious before God, but rather encouraging the free exercise of religion in every society. The dignity of the human person, proclaimed by Christian revelation, demanded it. But this *Declaration* merely confirmed what had been said in the *Church in the Modern World*—that the scientific search for truth, the political and social struggles for freedom and justice, the common striving of all human beings for a universal community have been embraced by the Church as *part of its own service* to the world. Christ's message is a transvaluation of the values of the world; the Church is his servant.

A Shift in Sensibilities

In the years that followed the Council, each successive pope has administrated the Church's heritage with renewed zeal. Paul VI continued John's gestures of openness to other Christian traditions, traveled widely throughout the world to show the Church's international character and its concern for justice. If his reforms of bureaucracy seemed too slow, his personal appointments to important posts and his increase of Third World representation balanced the delay. Recent popes have reduced papal pomp and circumstance, speaking no longer of *our,* but *my* positions in letters. Pope John Paul I (1978), during his brief time in office, rejected use of the tiara and described his first Eucharist as the inauguration of his ministry as supreme pastor rather than as a coronation. Papal coresponsibility meant service, not power.

These are shifts in sensibilities that the Council has promoted in Catholic life. The constant call by popes for social reform in recent encyclicals (*On the Progress of Peoples,* 1968; *The Redeemer of Humanity,* 1978; *Rich in Mercy,* 1980; *On Human Work,* 1981)

142

repeats the demands of predecessors since Leo XIII for the valuation of individuals, the dignity of labor, and the political development of repressed peoples. Implementations of the internal affairs of the Conciliar renewal have been no less enterprising, particularly in the development of lay ministries (catechists, readers of Scripture, ministers of Eucharist to the sick, and in some countries a host of others).[6] The establishment of a portion of the clergy who are married (men who are permanently deacons) has made it possible for the Church to see that ministerial service in the Catholic community need not be limited to the celibate. Sufficient change has occurred so that in some places, women, particularly those from religious communities, administrate parishes, operate in marriage courts and diocesan chanceries, and establish effective political lobbies.

Catholic life since the Council has indeed changed—perhaps no more so than in the sense of individual conscience which has emerged—largely through the negative reaction of Catholics in developed Western countries to the papal letter *On Human Life* (1968). After considerable discussion, Paul VI decided to repeat previous teaching which prohibited the use of artificial contraception to limit births. Because some clergy anticipated a reversal and the post conciliar commissions divided their recommendations, many hoped for change. The pope could not see that a consensus had been reached and maintained the previous position. The international dissent was clearly audible. Recent studies indicate that Catholic couples and the priests who counsel them regularly disagree with the papal position. The delicate question of the moral teaching authority of the papacy and its weight for hierarchies and for individual Catholics is at stake.

For just as surely as it is possible to dissent from papal teaching on ethical matters in sexuality, so, too, Catholics may question positions on social justice, just wages, the dignity of work, and international cooperation. If, largely negatively, some Catholics discovered that their consciences were their own through *On Human Life,* what prohibits utterly subjective decisions in social, political, and international affairs? So Pope Paul VI's eloquent cry for peace at the United Nations ("war never again") will be rejected unless clear criteria for conscience, theological and personal dissent, and unquestioning adherence to authority are reexamined. Many national episcopal conferences as well as the International Theological Commission itself are engaged in just such discussions.

The problem of ethical and theological dissent reflects signs of an international community redefining itself in local terms. Pope John Paul II has praised the spiritual heritage of ancient cultures like the Chinese, recalling the work of adaptation carried on by Jesuits in the sixteenth century (February 1981). It is possible, he maintained, to be truly Christian and authentically Chinese, since the Church's call is to service and not political colonialization. Yet attempts by the Dutch bishops to develop multiple lay ministries for the local Church, out of necessity as well as policy, met with considerable papal caution for the preservation of clerical difference (January 1981).

The final moving images of Pope John Paul II remain something of a blur—imperishable energy which propels him away from Europe toward Middle and South America, Africa, Japan, Mexico, and the United States; a photomontage of a pope with native American headdress, sombreros, baseball caps, and sunburned bare head; a preacher whose affecting cry for land reform, redistribution of wealth for the poor, and the dignity of the human person focuses the attention of nonbeliever and believer alike; a simple faithful human being whose body bleeds with an assassin's bullet. Pope John Paul II is convinced that the energetic exercise of his moral authority is Christ's gift to the role of Peter's headship in the Church. He intends to use it to establish the Christian humanism of which his predecessor Paul VI spoke.

Sergei Eisenstein (1898–1948), the Russian film producer, director, and critic, has argued that the constant splicing of images into a montage, the sheer juxtaposition of different aspects of reality, creates not only a new truth, but simultaneously a way to the truth.[7] John Paul II, the first non-Italian pope since the Renaissance, with his gift for languages, by his pilgrimages to every land, wishes to comprise in himself the diverse character of contemporary Catholicism. Seeing him allows Catholics to envision the presence of their unity in Christ. This shift from an abstract, universally uniform Church to a community everywhere available in indigenized particular or local churches will require many decades of ecclesiastical leadership.

Councils are always ends as well as beginnings. This ingathering of Catholics concluded a lengthy historical development in which the community began to turn toward the contemporary world of enlightenment, revolution, and the sciences. It starts an era in which the Church must unlock the treasures of its beliefs, rituals, and moral principles for the individualized attention of a multiplicity of cultures without losing its identity as precisely Christian. There are, of course, signs that the fearful would prefer to return to the old uniform Christendom, however narrow and discredited in the contemporary world; but Catholics in the United States and in the Third World, who now make up by far the majority within the Church, preach in differing tongues. "You can't go home again," as Thomas Wolfe has told us.

Vatican Council II proposed a new image for the Church—a pilgrim people, who like their master, Jesus, have no place to lay their heads. The hope for the future of Catholics lies in their ability to see themselves on a journey toward the Lord who comes to greet them, not in waiting behind closed doors for his arrival. The New Pentecost has propelled the Church into a future from which there is no return.

NOTES

1. Susan Sontag, *On Photography* (New York: Farrar, Straus & Giroux, 1978), 9–11.
2. George Tyrell, *Christianity at the Crossroads* (London: Longmans, Green & Co., 1909), 5.
3. Ibid., 275.
4. J. Derek Holmes, *The Papacy in the Modern World* (New York: Crossroad, 1981), 116.
5. Ibid., 208.
6. See David Power, *Ministries That Differ: Lay Ministries Established and Unestablished* (New York: Pueblo, 1980).
7. See Sergei Eisenstein, "The Film Sense," in *Film Form and The Film Sense,* trans. Jay Leyda (New York: World, 1967), 32.

FURTHER RELATED MATERIAL

Besides texts mentioned in chapter 9, Alec Vidler's *A Variety of Catholic Modernists* (New York and Cambridge: Cambridge University Press, 1970) is insightful and largely fair. J. Derek Holmes, *The Papacy in the Modern World* (New York: Crossroad, 1981) is an excellent description of the period from the institutional perspective. An entertaining, informative reading of the developments of Vatican Council II may be found in Xavier Rynne (pseudonym) *Letters from Vatican City: Vatican Council II (First Session)* (New York: Farrar, Straus & Giroux, 1963). Avery Dulles, in *The Dimensions of the Church* (Westminster, Md.: Newman, 1967), gives helpful reflections on the Church from the point of view of the Council. The recent volume by the same author, *A Church to Believe in: Discipleship and the Dynamics of Freedom* (New York: Crossroad, 1982), offers comments on the problem of the teaching authority of the episcopal office and the work of theologians.

11

THE CREATORS OF TWENTIETH-CENTURY CATHOLICISM (II) The United States and Religious Freedom

> Christ, fowler of street and hedgerow
> of cripples and the distempered old
> —eyes blinded as woodknots
> tongues tight as immigrants—
> takes in His gospel net
> all the hue and cry of existence.
> Heaven, of such imperfection,
> wary, ravaged, wild?
> Yes. Compel them in.
>
> Daniel Berrigan (b. 1921), from "The Face of Christ"

In March 1788, Catholic priests of the former British colonies petitioned Pope Pius VI (1775–99) for a bishop. They asked that he have power in his own right, that they choose the city in which the diocese would be established, and that they elect by ballot the individual most qualified. In July their requests were granted. On 18 May 1789, John Carroll (1735–1815) became first Bishop of Baltimore by a vote of twenty-four to two. Carroll planned that all future ecclesiastical organization in the new country would be patterned on this first appointment. The experiment of the Catholic Church with modern democratic processes of government had begun.

When this bishop became head of the Catholic missions in the United States, his pastoral care extended from Maine to the Carolinas and claimed territory from the Atlantic seaboard to the Mississippi River. Yet this was only a portion of the diverse Catholic population that constituted the American Church. To the original Spanish settlements in the Southwest and on the Pacific coast were added the French and British fur traders and trappers of the Midwest; the English Catholics of Maryland and Kentucky from which

147

Carroll emerged; the Irish, Italian, and Slavic immigrants of the later urban expansions; the Ukrainians, Armenians, and Greeks, with their non-Western liturgical languages; and the black Catholic slaves and shareholders in the South. *Diversity* of class, race, country of national origin, language, and region of settlement has always marked the Catholic Church in the United States.

There have been three fundamental stages in the Catholic institutional development: from the colonial period through 1830; from 1830 to 1960, in which enormous immigration solidified into a common Church; and from the turbulent 1960s with the entrance of the Second Vatican Council (1962–65) until the present. A *startling rise in the Catholic population* from the colonial period (a mere .03 percent) until the present (over 20 percent) has also characterized Catholic history in the United States.

Despite the Church's origins in Europe, its financial and ecclesiastical support from Rome, and its youth (a foreign mission until 1908), it has developed its own temperament. Its internal experiment with democratic politics grew into problems with Roman authoritarianism in the later nineteenth century. Its distance from the colonial seats of government made its citizens pragmatic. They "made do" with solutions that poor communications, insufficiently educated authorities, and personal inadequacy required.

Moreover, they had to wrestle with the fundamental Enlightenment principles that guided the founders of the Republic. Benjamin Franklin (1706–90), John Carroll's political supporter, stressed the mundane virtues: thrift, hard work, prudence, honesty, and moderation. Individual initiative, joined in a government by consent, was the basis for progress. Thomas Paine (1737–1809), the religious and political journalist, proposed a reasonable religion and detected Christianity's superstition, cruelty, and rational incomprehensibility. Thomas Jefferson's (1743–1826) interest in Christian experience was largely through an adherence to a useful moral code from which the confessional controversies and supernatural events had been removed. George Washington (1732–99) announced to Joel Barlow (1754–1812), then ambassador to Tripoli: "The government of the United States is not in any sense founded on the Christian Religion."

Separation of Church and state and the consequent religious tolerance enshrined in the first amendment to the American Constitution of 1788–89 did not establish a particular confessional Tradition, but neither did it encourage any "godly" affiliations. The antagonisms which had animated Church-state relations in Europe were not officially condoned; yet attainment of a mutual respect among pluralistic Christian, non-Christian, and areligious traditions had to be achieved through the dialogue of a common history. American Catholicism has been "on its own." As John Carroll remarked in 1783: "In these United States our religious system has undergone a revolution, if possible, more extraordinary than our political one."[1]

CATHOLIC DIVERSITY—ALWAYS PRESENT

The diverse origins of the Church in the Americas have marked every successive generation of Catholics. There have remained Catholic Christians whose native language is not English, but some other European tongue: French, Spanish, Polish, Italian, Czech, Hungarian, German, or Portuguese. Each national group faced isolation from its cultural roots, the aggressive missionary character of previous landholders, and the internecine repercussions of European conflicts on this side of the Atlantic. The three major colonial groups, joined by the mid-nineteenth-century immigrants and their twentieth-century counterparts, arrived for somewhat different reasons—and their religious identity reflects these original goals.

The Spanish Conquerors

Church and state arrived together in 1493 when Puerto Rico was claimed by Columbus for the King and Queen of Aragon and Castile. While the soldiers' primary objective was exploitation of the soil's resources, especially precious metals, Franciscan missionaries settled stable villages in which largely nomadic native tribes could be socialized to European culture and religion through education, vocational training, and codes of manners. The attachment of local Indians to the missions varied; most were virtually indentured serfs, all were loyal second-class citizens of the crown. The most difficult problems for the missionaries were the constant threat of force used by civil authorities and the ugly moral example given by exploring adventurers.

149

What once was merely a survival of religious place names in the Southwest, Texas, and Florida (St. Augustine, 1565; Santa Fe, 1609), has become again a Catholic heritage with which to reckon. Legal and illegal Hispanic immigration from Mexico, Cuba, and strife-torn El Salvador and Guatemala; the Puerto Rican population in New York City and northern New Jersey; and the migrant laborers in almost all agricultural states have reestablished this once-strong colonial force. By the year 2000, it is estimated that Hispanic Catholics will comprise at least half the ecclesiastical population in the United States.

Growing numbers, however, are not the only factor. The deep sense in which religion, culture, and language are intertwined in personal and familial identity is quite distinct from the northern European voluntary experience of religious belonging. Yet prior to the appointment of Robert Sanchez as archbishop of Santa Fe (1974), there had been no bishops of Hispanic origin since colonial times—and little official interest in integrating this culturally distinct religious experience.

The Piety of French Explorers

The primary objective of the French who appeared in 1604 off the coast of northern Maine was to establish a fur trade. They were in constant opposition to the English merchants to the south who established rival military forts. The native Americans of the region (Mohawks, Hurons, Oneida, Algonquin, and others) were used in these European rivalries to brutalize one or another of the parties involved. Throughout the seventeenth century, Jesuits such as Isaac Jogues (1607–47) valiantly contributed their lives to missionary activity among the Indians.

Just as Franciscans followed the Spanish explorers, or led the way as did Junipero Serra (1713–84) in California, so the Jesuits collaborated with French expeditions in the Midwest. Jacques Marquette (1637–75) accompanied Louis Joliet (1645–1700) down the Mississippi River (1673); and in the early eighteenth century, New Orleans was founded as its port. The trade in brandy, prostitution, arbitrary treatment of Indians, and the immoral example set by European Christians made missionary work extremely difficult in French territories.

Yet the French factor in Catholic life remains more than in a few place names (Detroit, 1701; Vincennes, 1702). In this and the last century, farmers and traders immigrated into northern New England, increasing and solidifying what remained of the old French population. New Orleans continues to be a "Catholic oasis" in what are otherwise the largely Protestant southern states. Remainders of Jansenist piety, strong familial loyalties, and a certain anticlericalism born of the Enlightenment continue to perdure in this cultural segment of Catholicism.

English Dissenters

The Catholic most Americans remember is not Juan de Padilla (about 1500–1544), Spanish Franciscan missionary to Kansas and the first American martyr (1542–44), but the English Lords Baltimore (George, 1580–1632; Cecil, 1605–75; and Charles Calvert, 1632–1715). Exhausted by the wars and mutual persecutions of the Christian communities of Europe, these aristocratic settlers came to Maryland just as their Pilgrim, Puritan, and Quaker counterparts did—to seek religious freedom. They proved to be the earliest and most formative influence upon Catholicism in the United States.

The mixed religious situation of the English colonists included Calvinist and antipapal Protestants. They saw themselves as the New Israel, a missionary community between the vice of French Catholic marauders to the north and Spanish papist adventurers to the south. The classic by Nathaniel Hawthorne (1804–64), *The Scarlet Letter,* describes some of the moral and political conflicts in these colonies. Though martyrs to religious anger were rare, the anti-Catholicism that characterized European controversies continued to mark some strains of American Protestantism. Even in Maryland itself, it was only in the early years, when Catholics controlled the government, that universal religious toleration was permitted—in fact, permitted for the first time anywhere.[2]

Maryland, like all the English colonies, was not founded to provide financial support in gold or furs to the home government—but to offer ports in which exported goods could be sold. As the colonies became more prosperous, able to provide home-manufactured goods for their own purposes and less dependent upon Britain for the maintenance of money and population (women were always a scarcity in the early days), rivalries began to develop in the politically dependent relationship.

During the prerevolutionary years, Catholics by the name of Carroll in Maryland and Brent in Virginia were wealthy landowners, though Protestants were always in the majority in both colonies. In this agricultural society, priests and lay Catholics owned black slaves as early as 1634, continuing a pattern which only ceased after the Civil War of the 1860s. These families and their servants were served largely by Jesuits who numbered a little over twenty for the entire region. The city of Philadelphia provided Catholicism with its only urban home in the colonial period; its congregation numbered (1733–34) about twelve hundred Irish, English, and German parishioners.

Colonial Catholics found themselves on both sides of the controversy for independence—but primarily on the side of revolution. Charles Carroll (1737–1832), denied enfranchisement for his Catholicism, despite the fact that he was clearly the wealthiest individual in Maryland, nonetheless threw himself into the fight for freedom. As he said in his later memoirs: "When I signed the Declaration of Independence, I had a view not only of our independence of England but the toleration of all sects, professing the Christian religion, and communicating to them all great rights."[3] The city milieu of wartime Philadelphia offered some Protestants their first experience of Catholics who were not Spanish enemies.

In a manner which Europeans would have found almost unimaginable, American Catholics embraced the strict separation of Church and state as the surest way to guarantee both political and religious freedom. A pattern had been set: Catholics in the United States did not need to theorize about the values or faults of "secular" separation. Rather they lived it first; and through that experience, they found it both useful and providential for ecclesial growth.

An Immigrant Church

The nineteenth-century ecclesial narrative consolidated the gains of religious toleration won with the revolution and welcomed the millions of immigrants who arrived after 1830. Some of these groups were fleeing political and religious oppression. The Irish, for example, were leaving their native land, not only because of the potato famines (1820, 1845–49), but also because of the centuries-old repression directed against their national Catholic identity. German Catholics fled from the growing secularizations of Otto von Bismarck's (1815–98) unification of Germany (the *Kulturkampf* of the 1870s). At the end of the century (1880–1920), Italian, Polish, Hungarian, and Slavic Catholics poured into the Churches of the United States, well over a million people a year. Throughout the century, indeed even to the Second World War, the Catholic minority formed the laboring class and city dweller, the undereducated occupants of foreign ghettos.

Each successive group of immigrants met with some opposition not only from non-Catholics but from older established Catholic communities as well. Those of French and English origin had a major problem. How could a single society, a unified national religious body, really absorb such diverse, sometimes contradictory, cultural and ethnic elements into itself?

A successful integration, which simultaneously permitted the religious expression of cultural diversity, was the remarkable achievement of astute nineteenth-century American bishops. Their objective was twofold: to help disoriented peoples maintain their Catholic heritage within a pluralistic and regularly hostile Protestant society, and to enable them to respect, identify with, and preserve the values of an alien culture. Ecclesiastical, educational, charitable, social, and moral institutions became avenues for immigrants to maintain religious difference, to preserve cultural customs, and to achieve independence within a highly competitive political society.

The Expanding-Contracting Church

As early as 1829, American bishops announced the necessity of establishing schools to educate the young in literacy, morality, and faith. At the end of the century, such local parish education became a norm and the ideal: every Catholic child in a Catholic school. This extraordinary institutional commitment, unlike any other in the world, was initiated, supported, and maintained by the voluntary financial, personal, and political generosity of Catholics, especially religious women. In 1808, Elizabeth Ann Seton (1774–1821), the first native-born American to be declared a saint (1975), began a school for women in Baltimore; in Emmitsburg, Maryland, she and her small community opened the first free parochial school for both sexes in 1810. It was a prophetic way to begin the century, since it was this educational system that, until the last quarter of our century, has formed Catholic identity.

The institutional preservation of the religious Tradition was an authentic way of conserving the Catholic experience in a westward-expanding country. Bishops like Carroll of Baltimore; Benedict Joseph Flaget (1763–1850) of Bardstown and Louisville, Kentucky; Matthias Loras (1793–1858) of Iowa, Minnesota, and the Dakotas; Peter Kenrick (1806–96) of St. Louis; and the extraordinary Jean-Baptiste Lamy (1814–88) of Santa Fe, memorialized in Willa Cather's (1873–1947) novel, *Death Comes to the Archbishop* (1927), extended the organization of the Church well beyond the cities of the Atlantic.

Without this institutional protection, it is unlikely that the growing storms of anti-immigrant, anti-Catholic sentiment might have been weathered. The "American Experiment" of religious tolerance for all confessional Traditions was weakened by Protestant hatred for papist superstition and a nativist fear of foreign domination. Catholic leaders soon found themselves forced to organize their people economically and politically in order to counter the signs of the times: "No Irish need apply." Horace Bushnell (1802–76), author of theological liberalism among American Protestants, summed it up in 1847: "Our first danger is barbarism; Romanism next."[4]

The language of the age was violent and abusive. Nativist and American Republican ("Know-Nothing") Parties sprang up (1840–50) controlling both Philadelphia and New York. Priests were tarred, feathered, and ridden on rails; 6 August 1855 became Bloody Monday in Louisville, Kentucky, when some twenty people were killed and hundreds wounded. The strong political colors of anti-Catholicism faded in the more serious controversies over slavery, but Abraham Lincoln (1809–65) remarked late the same month: "As a nation we began by declaring that all men are created equal. We now practically read it: All men are created equal except Negroes. When the Know-Nothings obtain control, it will read: All men are created equal except Negroes, foreigners and Catholics."[5]

These struggles within the American Experiment made bishops extraordinarily cautious in their statements about the slavery question. Some (as for example, Martin J. Spalding, 1810–72, of Louisville) identified abolitionism with Protestant bigotry. Indeed, there was midcentury Nativist propaganda that described slavery as the "natural coworker" of Roman Catholicism.[6] But more often, the questions and answers of slavery were not focused by religious principles, but economic and geopolitical ones. Catholic theologians, like Francis P. Kenrick (1796–1863), bishop of Philadelphia, regretted the consequences of slavery but emphasized that the public law must be obeyed. Catholics wanted to fit into a society that was aggressively trying to reject them.

Despite the fact that Pope Gregory XVI (1831–46) had condemned the slave trade as evil (1838), Catholics in the larger cities who competed with blacks for low-paying jobs ignored the slavery question. Only rare individuals, like Archbishop John Purcell of Cincinnati (1833–83), issued a call for emancipation at an official level. After the Civil War, the Second Plenary Council of the American bishops in Baltimore (1866) decreed that freed slaves were to be evangelized. But it was because Pope Pius IX asked an English priest, Herbert Vaughn (1832–1903), to send the Mill Hill Missionaries to the United States that schools, parishes, and a seminary were finally opened. Augustine Tolton (1854–97), born a slave, was the first acknowledged black priest in the United States. Ordained in Rome in 1886, he was meant for Africa; but the Roman congregation returned him to the United States. Said the cardinal in charge: "America has been called the most enlightened nation. We will see if it deserves that honor." Tolton ministered as a priest in Quincy, Illinois amid some clerical opposition. He died in Chicago as a pastor.[7]

The cost of these early, dramatic struggles of institutional Catholicism in America was not inconsiderable. So committed were the energetic talents of its finest leaders to the task of survival that other more important issues (like the question of slavery) were simply left untended. American Catholicism proved itself utterly capable of practical institutional genuis—building hospitals, orphanages, schools, churches, and social organizations. But toward what end?

Was the Catholic Church in this country to remain forever a triumph of buildings and boundaries, institutionally powerful, but intellectually and prophetically weak?

THE BREAKDOWN OF CATHOLIC
DEFENSIVE POSTURE: PRESIDENT AND POPE

When Alfred E. Smith (1873–1944), governor of New York and presidential candidate for the Democratic Party in 1928, was defeated, it was widely believed by Catholics that it was due to the sharp rise in anti-Catholic bigotry during the campaign. This sometimes angry, often disappointed, defensiveness gave way only in 1960 when John F. Kennedy (1917–63) was elected by a narrow margin to the presidency of the United States. Catholics felt as though they had come of age.

To pry Catholics free from their "separate but superior" culture, however, it had taken participation in two World Wars, committed pastoral support during the Depression of the 1930s, and a general leveling of American social distinctions brought on by both events. Non-Catholics discovered that Catholics were committed to the historic separation of Church and state. Catholics began to see that it was possible to be progressive, tough, and pragmatic in politics. Defensiveness was needless.

The combination of John Kennedy's election (1960) and the election of John XXIII to the papacy at about the same time (1958) allowed Catholics to feel secure, expansive, and free to commit themselves to societal and religious change. As the conciliar documents emerged, Catholics were being asked to rethink their relationship to the Catholic culture which had nourished them, protected them, and built up their confidence in a pluralistic world. Religious freedom had a purpose—service of society. Catholics began to search their American past—not for institutional precedents, but for prophetic leaders.

AMERICAN CATHOLIC PROPHETS

American Catholics discovered that there was a long Tradition of men and women who were not quite willing to let institutional

156

solutions settle public issues. Their attempts to mold a rapidly expanding, multinational Church should not so much be paralleled to the uniform cultural norm of the Carolingian or Constantinian Churches, but to the ensoulment of a quite new being.

Orestes Brownson (1803–73)

Brownson, a man of multiple literary talents and acerbic wit, found Catholicism after a lengthy trek through various American religious wildernesses. With his conversion at forty-one, he continued publication of the most original "personal" journal in Catholic history—*Brownson's Quarterly Review*. Although he was utterly convinced that the Catholic Church was the fulfillment of United States ideals, his criticism of parochial schools and immigrant Catholics, of despotic rule in the Papal States, his almost unique espousal of antislavery Unionism in 1860, and his hostility to Jesuits made his journal a constant source of irritation in midcentury Catholicism. Refusing either intellectual dependence or religious laxism, he spoke for both Catholic identity and democratic ideals in a period in which neither were honored.

Isaac Hecker (1819–88)

Hecker's personal religious quest led him through Ralph Waldo Emerson (1803–82) to a lecture of Brownson's which converted him to Catholicism (1844). Upon returning to the United States after his training by a German-speaking religious community, he traveled, successfully giving revivals. The community he founded, the Congregation of Missionary Priests of St. Paul (the Paulist Fathers), specialized in the communication of the Catholic experience in the United States. They founded the journal *Catholic World* (1865) and began a tract society which concentrated on appealing, intelligent, apologetic literature. In his own books (*Questions of the Soul,* 1855; and *Aspirations of Nature,* 1857), Hecker maintained his belief that Catholicism and democratic ideals could be synthesized.

John Ireland (1838–1918)

Ireland, the archbishop of St. Paul, Minnesota, spoke to French Catholics in mid-1892 with characteristic American optimism, enthusiasm, and activist concern. He urged priests to learn from their counterparts in the United States and leave their privileged positions to mingle with their congregations. Ireland rapidly found that his positions on the formation of conscience, the separation of Church and state, and the genuinely new legal experience of American politics were questioned. In 1897, when a French translation of Isaac Hecker's biography was published in Paris with an introduction by Ireland, it became the catalyst for a division of the French Church between republicans and loyalists.

In 1899, Leo XIII issued an encyclical (*Testem Benevolentiae*) which condemned "Americanism," warning against doctrines which came from the United States to Europe. As James Hennesey has remarked: "Something of a deep freeze set in, deepened further in the new century by Roman condemnation of Modernism."[8] But Ireland always remained a speaker for another way.

Prophets of Labor: John Gibbons (1834–1921) and John A. Ryan (1869–1945)

There can be no question but that American history would be different without the interventions of John A. Ryan and Cardinal John Gibbons of Baltimore. Just as the end of the nineteenth century saw Protestant theology writing and revising its social response to the Gospel in Walter Rauschenbusch (1861–1918), so Catholics could not ignore the political dimensions of squalor and oppression which accompanied the explosions of immigration and industrialization.

The Knights of Labor was the nation's first large union, founded by Uriah Stevens (1821–82) and headed after 1878 by Terence Powderly (1849–1924), a Catholic. Strikes and the Chicago Haymarket Riots (1886) frightened Catholics and Protestants alike. Through the support of Gibbons, the country's archbishops did not unilaterally condemn the movement as "socialist" or "communist"; and in a private visit to the Vatican, Gibbons assured Rome that its large Catholic constituency would not become radicalized.

Gibbons condemned child labor and urged the implementation of Leo XIII's encyclical *Rerum Novarum* (1890) on the living wage and just working conditions. With Ryan, Gibbons helped found the National Catholic War Council (NCWC) with its commitment to social and political action. After the First World War, the Council's commitment to social responsibility remained; and in 1919, it issued the "Bishops' Program of Social Reconstruction," written by Ryan. He advocated governmental employment offices, housing, pay scales, and an argument for a minimum wage. "Women who are engaged at the same tasks as men should receive equal pay for equal amounts and qualities of work."[9] He spoke in favor of industrial cooperation between workers and management. With some considerable difficulty, the Council became a permanent body of the American Church after the war: the National Catholic Welfare Conference (1922) and now the United States Catholic Conference.

When Franklin D. Roosevelt (1882–1945) was elected in 1933, Ryan welcomed the policies of the administration since they seemed to embody the very concepts of social justice for which he had argued. Ryan was at the NCWC from 1919 to 1945, and in charge of the social action aspects of the episcopal program from 1928. He never ceased to speak for social justice.

Dorothy Day (1889–1980)

If Hecker and Ireland spoke for American democracy and mystical Catholic freedom, Brownson for an intellectual Catholicism, and Gibbons and Ryan for labor, Dorothy Day spoke for the poor. On 1 May 1933, the first issue of the *Catholic Worker* was sold in New York City. In her religious autobiography, *The Long Loneliness* (1952), Day outlined the spiritual odyssey which drew her to Catholicism, despite her radical commitments to socialism, communism, and the American labor movement. It was only after meeting Peter Maurin (1877–1949), itinerant preacher for simplified life, justice, and community, that she saw how her commitments to social causes could be resurrected within the Catholic intellectual and religious Tradition.

With extraordinary dedication both to the institutional Church (the "cross on which Christ was crucified") and to the poor, Day inspired the foundation of Catholic Worker Houses across the country. They offer hospitality to all those who are in need. Day's contribution was not only to offer financial assistance, food, and clothing, but even the very privacy to which she might have been entitled. That was what it meant to share the life of the poor. As a pacifist, she condemned all wars, participating in antinuclear demonstrations even in her final years. Ever a pilgrim in United States middle-class society, she pricked consciences and provoked minds. Through the Catholic Worker houses traveled most of the Catholics of this century who have become conscious of their commitment to a new social order. For her, as for all the greatest of Catholic prophets, prayer and action were never separated because they proceeded from an undivided heart.

Journals, Monks, and Media

There were, of course, many other lesser-known prophets, such as Archbishop John Neumann (1811–60), now a saint (1977), who welcomed the Haitian black woman Elizabeth Lange (about 1810–89) when she began the first congregation of black religious to educate black children. Or Virgil Michel (1890–1938), a Benedictine monk of St. John's Abbey, Collegeville, whose publication *Worship* (originally *Orate Fratres*) was the focus for the liturgical movement and its link with the social action of Dorothy Day and John A. Ryan. Or Bishop John Lancaster Spalding of Peoria (1840–1916), who won his plea for the foundation of a national Catholic University in 1889 and opposed through the New England Anti-Imperialism League the colonial wars in the Philippines and Cuba.

When Fulton J. Sheen (1895–1979), later bishop and director of the national contribution to the worldwide Catholic mission effort (The Propagation of the Faith), called for a "Catholic Renaissance" in 1929, he helped awaken a sleeping giant, one whose institutional narcissism had made it more attentive to its own battles than others. From then until 1960, with Sheen's "Catholic Hour" (1930s–1950s) as companion, Catholics began reading more widely, writing more thoroughly about their past and present. They had as a widely recognized scholarly basis *The Catholic Encyclopedia* (1905–14). Journals like the nineteenth-century *Catholic World* (1865) were joined by the Jesuit-sponsored *America* (1909), the lay-controlled *Commonweal* (1924), and the scholarly *Theological Studies* (1940). The Catholic Historical Society (1884), the Catholic Biblical Association (1936), the Canon Law Society of America (1939), and the

Catholic Theological Society of America (1946) contributed to a significant maturation in Catholics' self-understanding. Most prophets in American Catholic history were characteristically activists; but Thomas Merton (1915–1968), like the reluctant prophet Jonah, joined the others through becoming a contemplative monk, a Trappist at Gethsemani, Kentucky. After intriguing the country through his autobiography *The Seven Story Mountain* (1948), a chronicle of his wandering toward monasticism, he assimilated the Catholic religious and mystical Tradition and found his way into the silence of God. Upon "arrival," he discovered not only that others had preceded him, but that God turned him toward the problems of the social order that he had left. Prayer and silence offered him critical distance as well as the chance for complete immersion in civil rights, nonviolent pacifism, and antinuclear movements. "Today more than ever the Gospel commitment has political implications, because you cannot claim to be 'for Christ' and espouse a political cause that implies callous indifference to the needs of millions of human beings and even cooperate in their destruction."[10] Merton offered American Catholics a criticism of their complacency and a vision of a more compassionate world.

The Architect of Dialogue:
John Courtney Murray

The sages, soldiers of the ecclesiastical fortress, and holy men and women, by their dedication to the transformation of poverty, injustice, and cruelty, vocally propelled the Church into the center of public controversy. They were allowed to do so through the fundamental religious and secular freedoms that the United States permits. John Courtney Murray (1904–64) joined the progressive forces at the Second Vatican Council, not to baptize American experience nor to canonize assured results, but to confirm that the conversation would continue throughout the universal Church.

In the Council's *Declaration on Religious Liberty* (1965), the European community listened to the experience of one of its former dependent churches. Just as the Church must be free to serve Christ, so individuals must be invited, not coerced, into loyalty to the

Gospel. This fundamental freedom should be enshrined in civil constitutions and international agreements. This freedom cannot be
abrogated without detriment to the glory of God.

RELIGION AND CULTURE—
THE POLITICS OF SECULARITY

The religious, civil, and intellectual dedication of American Catholics has continued in the world of post-Vatican II Christianity. The
prophets of social reform, religious criticism, and activist involvement have not disappeared with the removal of the war in Vietnam (1962–75). American bishops themselves have spoken out on
civil rights, racism, agricultural conglomerates, nuclear disarmament, the Appalachian poor, international politics, and welfare
programs.

The genuinely conservative and authentically progressive forces in
American Catholicism are now engaged in serious dialogue. Such
debates are healthy; they indicate that values are at stake that control
human lives. In just what direction this national discussion will turn
is for the prophets to determine; that the Church is traveling is
evident. Major religious movements which attempt to recapture the
affective experience of Catholic life, like the charismatic renewal, the
revival of Catholic ethnic consciousness and its frank avowal of
cultural difference, the developing politics of lobbying groups like
NETWORK or Right-to-Life, the shifting administrative patterns of
diocesan life toward lay involvement, the lower economic support
for the Catholic school system simultaneous with the rise in commitment expected of parish members—all these promise vibrant,
energetic conversation within the American Church.

What they have in common is the attempt by Catholics in the
United States to face the secularity of their environment. The concrete
utility and versatile experience of the American Experiment continues to intrigue European Catholics. And if it has its blundering
moments in a too facile approval of political opportunism (as in the
anti-Semitism of Charles E. Coughlin [1891–1973], the radio priest
of the 1930s), it nonetheless seems able to recover, by its very
evangelical independence, a critical balance.

There can be little question that the most significant cultural force in our world is the spirit of modernity: the rational science born in the early modern period and the Enlightenment critiques of reason, history, politics, and religion. When these are combined with the industrial and especially electronic technology that dominates both recovery of the past and proposals for the future, the United States remains the place where this spirit manifests itself as a national destiny. Whether one is in rural America, the decaying cities of the old Northeast, or the rising population centers of the West and Southwest, the redistribution of wealth and welfare occurring in the United States reiterates in its geographical, political, and racial diversity the reigning international problems at the turn of the millennium.

Catholics in this country face this movement not as though it were an outside army with which they must contend by dint of arms, but as a force *within* their own self-understanding. They stand in a radically ecumencial fashion with all religious traditions in the world, whether Hindu, Buddhist, Jewish, or Moslem, and utter the fundamental religious question: Why be religious, Christian, at all? Can one be both committed to modernity and the Christian Tradition with intellectual clarity, personal honesty, and institutional humility?

Catholics refuse to collapse their experiential commitment to modern values into secularism—the ideology that *only* secular values are true. A mutually critical conversation between modernity and Christianity characterizes the contemporary situation. Having escaped the understandable but prolonged domination by European custom, the approach of American Catholics has become radical, though practical; theoretical, yet committed to experience; open and workable; long-range in its ideals, but pragmatic in its demands for explicit, short-range answers. This "realistic" approach to religious and secular affairs is not laxist complacency, bored capitulation, or angry separatism. It is the concrete attempt to find the *legitimate means* by which the evangelical seeds of the Spirit may grow in a new culture.

Pope John Paul II's visit to the United States (1979) highlighted both the radical diversity of the Church and its unity in the Gospel; its need to achieve a place for itself in the pluralism of American cultures and a critical distance in the formation of a new society.

Chastened by its participation in wars (like Vietnam) and rumors of wars (like Latin America), the Catholic Church's optimism about success has been dimmed, but not obliterated; its activism reshaped, but not erased. Its enthusiasm has diversified to represent the spectrum of its inner membership; its identity less adolescent, more mature.

The diversity no doubt seems chaotic to some—particularly to those for whom the uniform Catholic isolation of the past was home. But the pilgrim Church in this country, in keeping with its frontier spirit and the evangelical commands, has cast its lot with the vibrant conversation of the present in accord with the adage followed by Pope John XXIII: "In necessary matters, unity; on doubtful issues, liberty; but in all things, love."

NOTES

1. James Hennesey, *American Catholics: A History of the Roman Catholic Community in the United States* (New York and London: Oxford University Press, 1981), 4.
2. Ibid., 41.
3. Ibid., 59.
4. Ibid., 119.
5. Ibid., 126.
6. Ibid., 145.
7. Cyprian Davis, *The Church: A Living Heritage* (Morristown, N.J.: Silver-Burdett, 1982), 257–59.
8. *American Catholics*, 203.
9. Ibid., 229.
10. Henry Nouwen, *Thomas Merton, Contemplative Critic* (New York: Harper & Row, 1981), 57.

FURTHER RELATED MATERIAL

The best account at present of general American Church history is James Hennesey's *American Catholics: A History of the Roman Catholic Community in the United States* (New York and London: Oxford University Press, 1981). More general descriptions within the context of American Protestantism and culture may be found in Sidney E. Ahlstrom, *A Religious History of the American People* (New Haven, Conn.: Yale University Press, 1973) and Martin Marty, *Righteous Empire: The Protestant Experience in America* (New York: Dial, 1970).

12

THE CREATORS OF
TWENTIETH-CENTURY CATHOLICISM (III)
Third World Catholics:
Liberation for a Future

> I have looked upon a savagely potent countenance
> Of soft lines, of diverse directions.
> I have confronted it until it dissolved like cloud,
> And saw, behind, the true Countenance with no beginning or end.
> Eduardo Anguita (b. 1914) from "El Verdadero Rostro"

Maps tell us where we are. We use them to show us how to find our way to somewhere else. The first published maps from the European colonial expansion placed the cartographer's native country in the center of the earth with a distant, distorted Siberia, China, Australia, and Oceania on the far right and Alaska to the far left. The Pacific Ocean was divided.

These early drawings centered the world on its most important population centers. But if we were to take seriously the changes in demography since the sixteenth century, Rome and northern Europe would no longer be the center of our space. Most of the human beings of the third millennium will occupy an arc which extends between South America to Africa through the countries of southern Asia. Placing that crescent in the center of the map, Old Europe would be on the left edges, New England on the right—and the Pacific would have replaced the Mediterranean as the new inland sea. Even now, well over 50 percent of the world's population dwells in Asia, the new center of the known world.

Yet de facto shifts in population, as we know, are not necessarily changes in power. The old East-West matrix of authorities still dominates the economic and political structures of our world. Yet the fundamental crises facing the construction of a global humanity are now aligned along a North-South axis, where Europe, the United

States, and the Union of Soviet Socialist Republics comprise the North, and the southern hemisphere is the Third World.

The term "Third World" does not simply designate a region, but the economic, sociological situation of the massive numbers of people who live there. They are often resource-rich and finance-poor; they are exploited for their labor force, mineral deposits, or land and oppressed by oligarchic or multinational arrangements which preserve the status quo. Once dominated by European colonialism, they are now under great pressure from Soviet or American influence. In the wake of rising economic "development," they find themselves hostage to oil-producing countries (some developing nations themselves) who fuel their new factories. Economic imperialism has been no better than religious or nationalist colonialism. Resentment breeds anger and resistance; resistance breeds governmental instability and oppression; oppression breeds coups and revolutions.

What of the Catholic Church in this world of Asia, Africa, Middle and South America? As an explicitly international community, Catholicism sees the experience of these countries, however diverse, as a positive movement of the Spirit and waits to be taught their message. An explicit theology, rooted in the experience of suffering, poverty, and fear, has risen in the hearts and minds of Third World Catholics. It has stressed that God's future is with the poor and the disenfranchised. Catholics in countries of yellow, brown, red, and black peoples have become the visionaries of our religious future. European popes may have gathered a new Pentecost in the Second Vatican Council, and the United States bishops may have encouraged pluralism of expression, but the diversity of tongues that have responded is clearly from other worlds.

CATHOLICS IN ASIA—
THE MEANING OF TRANSCENDENCE

Asia is clearly the world's most religious continent. From its borders have emerged all three of the major world monotheisms, Judaism, Christianity, and Islam, as well as the major moral religions, Hinduism, Buddhism, Shintoism, and Confucianism. Asia contains 54 percent of the world's population, yet only 2.3 percent of it is Catholic. If we remove the Philippine peoples from that figure, then only .95 percent of the total belongs to the Catholic Church. Figures for the Protestant Churches are not significantly different.

In this least Christian environment, Catholics are largely a product of the evangelization efforts of Portuguese expansion. Their primary objective was to establish trading ports and protective fortresses, not to colonize inland territories. Catholics have maintained the same static presence, sponsoring schools and charitable institutions which house the poor and outcast. In India, conversion offered self-respect to the lowest castes and an exit to higher classes. In Japan, conversion meant incredible xenophobic persecution for two hundred years, rapid growth in the post-World War II period, and a 5 percent drop in the Catholic population every year since about 1960.

Why can Christianity not make a serious institutional or religious difference in East Asian life? Shusaku Endo (b. 1923), the Japanese novelist, remarks in *The Silence* (1969) that the religious vision of his nation is fundamentally different from that of the West—that it requires a vulnerable divinity whose compassion for human suffering and the ignobly oppressed appears as his most striking quality. The Christendom which transcends all countries and territories is fiercely powerful, proud, and demanding. The Christ Christians should witness is One who would have even denied his own divine mission out of love for bleeding humanity.

Others believe that it is the contemplation of Transcendence to which Christians must give testimony in their Asian missionary efforts. Like all Western activists, they founded schools, orphanages, and hospitals—important embodiments of the caring Tradition of Catholicism; but they failed to announce the gentle holiness that Buddhist monks proclaimed.

In no case is the witness of Asian Christians doubted. In Vietnam, during the long civil wars and struggles for independence, its Catholics were regularly persecuted; in Japan, Christians of all denominations were almost eradicated; and in China, there remained a nationalized Church after the 1948 Revolution, utterly dependent upon the state for survival, and an underground Catholicism of resistance to the government.

It is the *quality* of Transcendence to which Catholic Christians witness in East Asia that is at stake; it is the meaning of the Sacred announced by the Gospel of Jesus that requires new cultural delineation. But if the Church is to *listen* to the voices of Asian converts, it will hear new accents in its own understanding of God and the meaning of Christ. Catholics and Protestants in their common confrontation with secularization (now a prominent Japanese export) will comprise a new chorus.

AFRICAN CATHOLICS—THE JOY OF FAITH

Africa, although traveled by missionaries in the thirteenth century, remained largely a mystery to Europeans until 1900. The ancient Church of North Africa, which contributed so much in figures like Augustine (354–430) and Cyprian of Carthage (+258), was erased by the wars of Islam some four hundred years later. The colonial expansion of European powers carved the continent into areas of influence and exploited the population for the slave and ivory trades. It founded Catholic kingdoms like that of the native Affonso I (1506–45), whose realm stretched from the Atlantic to present day Kinshasa and south into what is now northern Angola. It is from this period that Christian symbols have remained an idiom of personal and social power in Zairean cultural heritage.[1]

No continent has been humiliated more than Africa through the colonial slave trade. The plight of millions in the Third World is riveted in the manacles which destroyed tens of thousands and imprinted scourges on the brains and the backs of Africans. Aimé Césaire (b. 1913), African politician and poet, states: "I am talking of millions of men who have been skillfully injected with fear, inferiority complexes, trepidation, servility, despair, abasement."[2]

Described in ethnological and exegetical nonsense as the accursed sons of Ham from the Book of Genesis (9:20–25), Africans can still feel their psychological servitude to missionaries. J. E. K. Aggrey (1875–1927) of Ghana cried: "My African people, we are created in God's image. They wanted us to think of ourselves as chickens, but we are eagles. Spread your wings and fly."[3]

In 1900, Africa contained two million Catholics; from 1952 until 1972, the African Church rose in population from twelve to thirty-six million believers. This missionary success seems to have originated not in colonial enterprise (it was a period of decolonialization) nor in stability of religious culture (it was the period of Vatican II), but in two other factors: the effectiveness of the missionary school and a deep religious predisposition of the African spirit.

Africa's Catholics embraced the conciliar *Constitution on the Liturgy* (1965) with enthusiasm, particularly its sections on cultural adaptation to local language, customs, and indigenous talent.[4] But the religious spirit of the people is not merely ritualistic; indeed, its deepest sense is of nature, the family, and tribal loyalty. The areas in which Catholicism has had its most difficult problems in evangelization in Africa are precisely those in which ordinary ecclesiastical law prohibited adaptation to cultural expression: polygamy and tribal initiation rites.

The original purposes of the missionary school, catechesis and service of the Church, have been undeniably successful. Unconsciously or consciously, however, these same goals have fostered personal achievement based upon competitiveness, migration from the original family or tribe, and the establishment of important voluntary groups, such as Church, political party, or national state. Such shifts are not intrinsically evil developments; but as Catholic missionary schools have become part of the national educational systems, they must be replaced by evangelization which stresses social conscience and duty to the common welfare.

When Paul VI visited Africa in 1969, he recognized the difficulties as well as the hopes of Catholic assemblies. When John Paul II celebrated a century of evangelization (1980) with Zairean Catholics, he did not anticipate that the Christian Gospel would collapse into the local culture, but that it would help "these cultures . . . bring forth from their own living tradition original expressions of Christian life, celebration and thought."[5] The Pope views Catholic inculturation into Africa as a work that will require lengthy discussion, spiritual discernment, and the liberation of those elements that announce the paschal mystery of Christ.

LATIN AMERICA—THE LOCAL CHURCH'S LIBERATION OF LOCAL SOCIETY

African Catholicism is a hopeful world where life seems omnipresent, even in its darkest depressions, as in Uganda in the mid-1970s or South Africa in the 1980s. Latin Catholicism is a world looking for hope. The waves of evangelization, first from the fifteenth to the

169

nineteenth century, then during the period of colonial liberation and European immigration (1800–1914), and finally into the present, have left the countries of Middle and South America poor, exploited, and Catholic largely by symbolic affiliation.

Spanish colonial empires brutally enforced a uniform cultural Christianity. Hispanic conquest rooted the authority of the religion and state in the towns, replacing the ruling classes (whether in Mexico or Peru). They spread in concentric circles, setting up plantations which gave the population of worker-Indians to the explorers, organizing village settlements even further away, and giving missions to Jesuits and Franciscan or Dominican friars who patrolled the edges of the empire.

Religion was the mark that separated the incorporated from the uncivilized. Christianity, built upon the rubble of ancient temples, replaced a state-controlled priesthood. Despite the small armies (Hernando Cortes [1485–1547] had 508 soldiers, 100 sailors; Francisco Pizarro [1471–1544] about 177 followers; friars in Mexico and Guatemala never exceeded one thousand), conversion to Catholicism defined civil loyalty.[6] In this post-Reformation world, attachment to local community (town, village, tribe) was intense; but religion, not language or race, was the distinguishing loyalty which founded the nation. With Spanish dominion came the Catholic religion.

The heirs to this social situation have largely been the ruling oligarchies, wealthy established families whose industries and political affiliations controlled the government, communications, armies, utilities, and—religion. It is a society based upon dependence, a paternalistic institution in which the children receive what remains. Leonardo Boff (b. 1938), the Brazilian theologian, has enumerated the symptoms of this dependence:

> Hunger, infant mortality, endemic diseases, cheap manual labor, deteriorating pay scales, abandonment of the schools by young people who must help their families eke out a living, a lack of participation and freedom, an inability to gain recognition of the most basic human rights, political corruption, and control of the nation's wealth by a small but powerful elite.[7]

In such a situation, the Catholic Church has chosen to speak the language of the oppressed. In the mid-1960s, Catholics recovered the voice of the local Church and its ability to criticize, on the basis of the Gospel, governmental and ecclesiastical leaders for their neglect of the disenfranchised. In 1964, Ivan Illich (b. 1926), now of Cuernavaca, Mexico, spoke at Petròpolis, Brazil, on the revision of pastoral strategies in the Latin American Church. Gustavo Guttierez (b. 1928) described theology as critical reflection upon the institutionalized violence of the governmental regimes. Guttierez's thought was refined in the ensuing years and was published as a fountainhead of later indigenous theology (*A Theology of Liberation*, 1973). Basing their work on the educational methods of Paulo Friere ([b. 1921], *Pedagogy of the Oppressed*, 1970) and listening intently to the experience of the revolutionary Ernesto Ché Guevara (1928–67) and Camilo Torres (1929–66), a priest who joined the guerrilla movement, Illich, Guttierez, and others began to offer an ecclesial perspective that was authentically of the Gospel, society, and the Third World.

After a period of trial and error, the Catholic Church of Middle and South America met at Medellín, Colombia (1968). Vatican Council II (1962–65) had spoken of the underdeveloped countries, the relationship of the Church and the world, and renewal. Medellín offered a vision of the planet from the standpoint of the poor countries, described the role of the Church in that world as liberation and provided guidelines for the transformation by the Church of a society living in misery and injustice.

When Pope John Paul II visited Middle and South America ten years later, he did not, as was sometimes misinterpreted by the public press, denounce the qualitative leap made at Medellín concerning the Church's role in the renewal of society. On the contrary, he spoke of a human dignity based upon the Gospel and the difficulties inherent in bringing that to specific configuration. In an address at Oaxaca, Mexico, he spoke of himself as the "voice of those who cannot speak or who have been silenced. It is not Christian to continue certain situations that are clearly unjust."[8]

For Pope John Paul, the local church is an authority. He usually chooses to confirm the direction taken in local episcopal conferences (except in Holland, as we have noted), only reminding them of their international responsibilities to the Gospel and their unity with the worldwide Church, symbolized through his office. In speaking to

Brazilian bishops a year later, he remarked that there must be an "affective" dialogue which will permit constant openness to the work of the Spirit in the local communities of God's people. This collegial Spirit on the local level will encourage active discussion of the concrete problems of the peoples who make up the Church. In this way, "the church can actually contribute to the transformation of society by helping it to become more just and to be founded on objective justice."[9]

THE THIRD WORLD AND CHURCH INVOLVEMENT

Since better than 70 percent of the Church's population will exist in Third World countries by the year 2000, and since that Church is, on the whole, utterly poor and extremely young, its growing sense of who it is and what it must do is of crucial importance to Catholicism. The local Church's involvement in political and social change and the international, even papal, support for such change is part of the response. The criticism of its theology and the fears for its social absorption or annihilation are equally significant.

The Programs

Formerly, the Churches of Asia, Africa, and the Americas south of the United States were the object of political, economic, and social maneuvers by others. Now, in their multicultural complexity, they have discovered that they can create themselves. But becoming conscious of the ability to make history as well as to suffer it means achieving an independence which is sometimes hesitant, often violent, and occasionally mistaken. In their attempts to develop self-renewing cultures, Third World countries have found it difficult to move beyond the common biases and successes of democratic liberalisms, autocratic socialisms, and repressive Marxisms. But their only concrete alternatives have been the unredeemed oppressions of present authoritarian governments. The choice has not been abstract—the "best of all possible governments."

The concrete task of the Church in the Third World has become to assist peoples in their search for the most liberating options in the situation. This regularly means education from nonliteracy to the visual and aural technology of contemporary communications

172

equipment, the replacement of numerous clerical missionaries from Europe or the United States by a few native lay ministers, and the establishment of political clout necessary to exchange poverty of land, medicine, and clothing for ownership of property, personal and familial health care, and food.

Nor can this work be seen as somehow alongside the Church's commitment to the Gospel. Though Christian faith contemplates the Kingdom of God first, the neighbor is the first citizen in the New Heaven and the New Earth. Asian Christianity's focus upon transcendence, Africans' joyful embrace of the giftedness of God's love, and Middle and South American emphasis on freedom meet in the Incarnate Word.

The human dignity of every individual, of tribal or national cultures, of international interdependence is the will of God as disclosed in Jesus who ate with the outcast, loved sinners, and lived with the poor. Jesus is not a "revolutionary in the emotional and ideological sense of violent and rebellious reaction against the sociopolitical structure. Perhaps a suitable description of Jesus would be Liberator of a consciousness oppressed by sin and all alienations and Liberator of the sad human condition in its relationships with the world, the other and God."[10]

The Plans—Theology of Liberation

The thought that has emerged from the confrontation of the Gospel with this Third World situation is often called the Theology of Liberation. It takes seriously two loyalties: to the Tradition of loving service proclaimed in Jesus of Nazareth and to the particular human situations in which theologians find themselves.

The original impetus came from the social encyclicals of popes, from Leo XIII's *Rerum Novarum* (1891) through Pius XI's *Quadragesimo Anno* (1931) to John XXIII's *Mater et Magistra* (*Mother and Teacher*, 1961), *Pacem in Terris* (*Peace on Earth*, 1963) and *Populorum Progressio* (*On the Development of Peoples*, 1967) of Paul VI. As historical documents, these papal letters acknowledged in unmistakable terms the responsibilities of Catholicism to the social order. They favored, rather than dreaded, the eventual socialization of economies. They asked, as a matter of justice, not charity, that the rich nations aid the poorer nations of the world. They denounced repressive regimes and called for the reform of social, economic, and political wrongs. They made it clear that religion could never be a merely private matter without public consequences.

This official Catholic teaching was encouraged by the beginning dialogue between Marxists and Christians. These unlikely conversation partners appeared on both sides as intrepid, conciliatory spirits, neither the Stalinist remains of an official Soviet ideology nor the Catholic dogmatic anticommunism of the Cold War period. On the one hand, the Marxists were revisionists, whose attitude toward Karl Marx (1818–83), the German revolutionary socialist and social and economic theorist, had shifted from his materialist critiques of history and his denunciations of religion as the alternative for concrete implementation of human freedoms. Catholic interest was sparked by the papal encyclicals and their personal concern for the authentic dignity of the human person.

The thinkers' common purpose—the liberation of humanity from all oppression and the removal of repressive societal structures—created a collaborative climate which has largely persisted. So Ernst Bloch (1885–1977), with his philosophy of hope leading to Utopia, the sociological critiques of Max Horkheimer (1895–1973) and Theodor Adorno (1903–69), and the social-critical philosophy of Jurgen Habermas (b. 1929) and the Frankfurt School promoted a milieu in which Christians and Marxists could study the phenomenon of society and religion together.

John Baptist Metz (b. 1928), a student and colleague of Karl Rahner (b. 1904), has offered perhaps the most coherent vision of this dialogue from the Catholic perspective. Metz is aware that concrete Marxist social legislation, whether in the Soviet Union, its satellites such as Poland or now Afghanistan, or even the more Stalinist forms of Eurocommunism, is utterly at variance with a Christian understanding of the world. Nonetheless, through conversation with these social and political thinkers, Metz wants to propose a precisely Christian theology of the *world*.

A religion privatized by the enthronement of the middle-class individual will not provide a theology that will serve the contemporary world. The whole project of the Church must be the achievement of a critical liberty of faith, not a nostalgia for the past traditions which might have embodied Catholic meaning. Metz stresses the primary role, not of concepts and doctrines, but of the liberating story, the critical character of a disturbing memory, and the concrete witness to that explosive memory of Jesus in the present. This theology is beyond mere self-reflection; it aims to change the world. It is beyond the neurotic assimilation of whatever political compulsion appears, and it is radically interdisciplinary in its search for the nonabstract solutions that will transform the world.

These notions have been expanded, repeated, and concretized for the Third World by many Latin American theologians: Gustavo Guttierez of Peru; the Brazilian Leonardo Boff ([b. 1938] *Jesus Christ Liberator,* 1972); the Uruguayan Juan Luis Segundo ([b. 1925] *A Theology for Artisans of a New Humanity,* 1971); the Argentine lay historian Enrique Dussel ([b. 1934] *Historia de la Iglesia en América Latina: Coloniale y liberación, 1492–1973,* 1974); the Chilean pastoral theologian Segundo Galilea ([b. 1928] *Espiritualidad de la liberación,* 1973); and many others equally persuasive and eloquent.

Some of these individuals are priests, some laymen and women. All are passionately convinced of the Catholic Church's role in the reversal of oppression and in its ability to found a new society. They all put a premium upon partisanship in the specific political debates of their countries; they do not believe in an abstract Christianity devoid of cultural embodiment. Grace must always be seen as on the side of one class or another. For them, involvement in what is true is a presupposition to discovering the truth of the Gospel in this world. The God of Christians is a constant Critic of society, the eschatological "No" to all limited or oppressive structures. His love will endure until the entire world is ultimately redeemed.

SPECIFIC STRATEGIES OF
WORLD TRANSFORMATION

Every thinker has his or her particular plan for the revolutionary changes required in Third World societies. Those committed to a Theology of Liberation are willing to trust to the dialogue of grassroots communities in the local Church, to the ecclesiastical debates about prudence and tolerance of difference, and to the political arguments which so easily sanction the status quo. What they are

unwilling to condone and tolerate is the abusive power which totalitarian governments use to destroy the conversation. And thus
they suffer.

So there are martyrs in Chile, Panama, and Argentina; the assassi-
nation of the archbishop in El Salvador. The rejection of either the
colonialisms of the past or the developmental neoimperialism of the
present has placed those who side with the poor in danger. Nor are
foreign missionaries immune: four church women from the United
States were brutally murdered in El Salvador and an Oklahoma
priest was killed at his Guatemalan Indian mission.

The Third World Churches are busily redefining their de-
centralized relationship to the international Church. A polycentric
world prohibits uniform legislation in all matters. Their ecumenical
activism, their use of grass-roots religious formation in education,
their concentration on family life and the redefinition of the lay-
clerical relationship mark the vibrant character of this Church.

When the Third World Church provides an example, a parable for
the entire Catholic community showing the intermediate procedures,
rules, offices, and processes for implementing its critique of society
and its renewed governance of the Church, it will have stepped
beyond being only a visionary, authentically apocalyptic criticism of
the present. The faithfulness of these believers to their particular
situations, a fidelity unto death, discloses to them and to the
worldwide community of Catholics an uncanny event—that the
ignored and despised, the betrayed, forgotten, and impoverished can
become the most human story of all.

NOTES

1. Crawford Young, *The Politics of Cultural Pluralism* (Madison, Wis.:
University of Wisconsin Press, 1976), 182–86.
2. Cited in Frantz Fanon, *Black Skin, White Masks* (New York: Grove
Press, 1967), 9.
3. Wahlbert Bühlmann, *The Coming of the Third Church,* trans. Ralph
Woodhall and A. N. Other (Maryknoll, N.Y.: Orbis, 1977), 151.
4. *Vatican Council II: The Conciliar and Post-Conciliar Documents,*
ed. Austin Flannery (Northport, N.Y.: Costello, 1975), 13–14.
5. *Origins,* vol. 10:1 (May 22, 1980), p. 5.
6. Young, *Politics of Cultural Pluralism,* 432–35.

7. Leonardo Boff, *Liberating Grace*, trans. John Drury (Maryknoll, N.Y.: Orbis, 1979), 84–85.
8. *Puebla and Beyond*, ed. John Eagleson and Philip Scharper, trans. John Drury (Maryknoll, N.Y.: Orbis, 1979), 294–95.
9. *Origins*, vol. 10:9 (July 31, 1980), p. 131.
10. Leonardo Boff, *Jesus Christ Liberator*, trans. Patrick Hughes (Maryknoll, N.Y.: Orbis, 1978), 240.

FURTHER RELATED MATERIAL

Overall surveys of Third World Church experience are rare. Wahlbert Bühlmann's *The Coming of the Third Church*, trans. Ralph Woodhall and A. N. Other (Maryknoll, N.Y.: Orbis, 1977) is still useful. Rosino Gibellini's *Frontiers of Theology in Latin America*, trans. John Drury (Maryknoll, N.Y.: Orbis, 1979) presents current programs or positions by contemporary Latin American theologians and social critics. Martin Jay's *The Dialectical Imagination: The History of the Frankfurt School and the Institute for Social Research, 1923–1950* (London: Heinemann, 1974) offers an overview of the recent social-political criticism which has generated the Marxist-Christian dialogue.

13

A CATHOLIC VISION

And though the world, at last, has swallowed her own solemn laughter
And has condemned herself to hell:
Suppose a whole new universe, a great clean Kingdom
Were to rise up like an Atlantis in the East,
Surprise this earth, this cinder, with new holiness!
  Thomas Merton (1915–68), from "Senescente Mundo"

Though educated in the pre-Vatican II church, Flannery O'Connor (1925–64), the irrepressibly Southern author, was convinced that Catholic vision must change. Like many 1950s believers, she knew that a "child's faith [was] all right for the children, but eventually you have to grow religiously as every other way.... What people don't realize is how much religion costs. They think faith is a big electric blanket, when, of course, it is the cross. It is much harder to believe than not to believe."[1]

She recommended a French Jesuit who inspired thinking Catholics with the confidence that it was possible to be committed both to the Tradition and to contemporary human and natural sciences. "He was a paleontologist—helped to discover Peking man—and also a man of God." For many contemporary Christians, this man who had spent his life hunting among rocks for signs of primitive humanity in Asia, South Africa, the United States, and Europe, a man who was forbidden by his Roman superiors to publish his religious reflections upon science during his lifetime, became a visionary prophet of Catholicism.

Pierre Teilhard de Chardin (1881–1955) worked as a medic during World War I, gained success as a geologist through his successive tours of China, and never ceased thinking through the scientific context and its consequences for Christian faith. What his theological writings lack in rigor, they gain in vision. As O'Connor remarked: "I don't suggest you go to him for answers but for different questions, for that stretching of the imagination that you need."[2]

Teilhard was herald of an age in which science and religion might become partners in a dialogue toward the rebuilding of the earth. In two of his most popular works (*The Phenomenon of Man*, 1959; *Divine Milieu*, 1960), he saw the universe developing ever greater systems of complexity. In this increasing spiral, quantum jumps occurred in consciousness, such as the emergence of humanity and the development of its self-conscious reflection. As a consequence of the incarnation of Jesus, the material universe is moving toward an ultimate point of intensification and convergence in Christ. What we must have to appreciate creation "is much less new facts (there are enough, and even embarrassingly more than enough of these in every quarter) than a new way of looking at the facts and accepting them. A new way of seeing, combined with a new way of acting: that is what we need."[3] The Lord of creation was witnessed by both science and religion.

The scientist trusted in the christological unity of faith and reason, Church and world, and by that conviction offered to Catholics a synoptic statement amid growing social and religious pluralism. The historical revivals (patristic, liturgical, biblical) revealed how multifaceted the Tradition had been. The post-World War II cultural differences of believers threatened the unity of Catholicism. Vatican Council II legitimated indigenous diversities in worship, practice, and the expression of belief. As a result, it is not uncommon to hear both active and disaffected Catholics asking themselves what characterizes the Church's identity. How do I know I am still Catholic? What focuses the kaleidoscopic explosion of diversity?

CATHOLICISM IS ITS TRADITION

The center of Catholic identity remains the faithful affirmation that God has acted in the past in Jesus of Nazareth proclaimed as the Christ when he gathered up in his words and work the people of Israel, that he acts in the present through the Spirit, and that he will continue to act in the future, transforming the universe until it is transparent to divine love.

Catholics believe that the faithfulness of God is rendered concrete in all history. They are convinced that it is decisively represented in the structure, sacraments, and preaching of the believing community. There the unique saving action of Jesus is disclosed anew in the authentic actions of the past and present, the official authorities and ministries within the church, and the worship of believers. In these social expressions, the incarnation of divinity in humanity has been extended until the end of history.

CATHOLICISM IS SACRAMENT

If the Catholic Church is its Tradition, it is not yet the Kingdom of God. To canonize its history would be stupid as well as blasphemous. To say that Tradition is the meaning of the Church is not to say that God does not show the divine reality in created nature. On the contrary, Catholics believe that in Jesus Christ both historical traditions and natural religious yearnings have their fulfillment. Jesus is both sign of what the world is to be and the historical reality of its Presence. He is Sacrament of our meeting with God.

The Church is the effective, though partial, presence of our encounter with this Christ. When the Church gathers in worship, it proclaims what it is and hopes to become: God's people graced by his love. The Eucharist, the central act of Catholic worship, may serve as an example of what we mean. In this sacramental celebration, the ordinary signs of sharing, of giving and receiving, of resolving conflict and alienation are crystallized in a meal of bread and wine. The quite standard fare—grains of wheat kneaded into a single loaf and grapes crushed to form one cup of wine—is gathered into the memory of a single individual. Nature is reshaped by history.

Marked forever by Jesus' words "This is my body; this is my blood," the simple elements disclose one in Whom Christians trust for the meaning of their lives and for the significance of the universe. The words spoken, the gestures made, the elements used do not merely remember the community. They continue to stand over against the believing assembly as a call to unity and peace, a challenge to love one another. Believers must become what they share— the Body of Christ.

Nature is caught up into a particular biography and reveals its authentically universal meaning; personal stories are challenged by the Word to become what they most want to be—forthright love without fear. For Catholics, this "great exchange" between the

181

Divine and the human occurs at crucial moments in their lives: birth and growth into maturity, the assumption of new tasks and roles in the community, personal and communal failure, sickness, and death. The seven sacraments—Baptism, Confirmation, Orders, Marriage, Reconciliation, the Sacrament of the Ill or Dying, and the Eucharist —are misunderstood if they are seen as natural magic or reduced to the merely subjective memory of wishful historical thinking. On the contrary, God's action for humanity in Jesus is so real and lasting that it abides as his gift in every dimension of our existence.

For Catholics, the sacraments are signs that effect what they signify. The natural signs of cleansing water, strengthening oil, nourishing food, the promising word, and reconciling or confirming hand are graphically specified in Christ's history of death and resurrection as his own inaugural baptism, his anointing Spirit, his table fellowship with sinners, his undying faithfulness to his people, his words of forgiveness, and his call to apostolic leadership.

In the course of Catholic history, these sacramental rituals have continually reshaped themselves according to the needs of the culture and the demands of the Gospel upon that particular society. But in all situations, Catholics believe that Christ remains present as transfiguring Lord through these signs prayed by the faithful community. Their effectiveness is the gift of God; their enactment is the task given believers.

SACRAMENT IS HISTORY—
THE CUMULATIVE INCARNATION

Just as the early history of a child marks its adulthood, so certain aspects of the Church's past remain part of its meaning. Embedded within the narrative we have related is a set of cumulative achievements and requirements of which an authentic vision of Catholicism must take account (see Fig. 1, p. 183).

If Catholics are faithful to their own past, they will always meet (1) their origins in image, symbol, and story, (2) their social and institutional embodiment in doctrines, creeds, and authoritative councils, (3) their diverse interpretations inviting systematic and theoretic thought. Yet (4) these progressive cultural embodiments would be pointless, if they ignored the salvation they seek to understand. The challenge of the prophets reminds the community that the

Figure 1

	(1) 100–300	(2) 300–600	(3) 600–1300	(4) 1300–1600	(5) 1600–1800	(6) 1800–1900	(7) 1900 . . . . C.E.
Influential Philosophers	Plato Aristotle Plotinus Proclus →			Nominalism William of Ockham →	Descartes Wolff →	Kant Schelling Hegel →	Kierkegaard Nietzsche Marx Heidegger →
History of Catholicism							
Questions Raised	Images Symbols Stories	Social Institutions	Reading Question Disputation *Summa*	Conversion History of Church Sin–Grace	Church-State Relations Religious Piety	History Method Praxis	Myth-Legend Modernity-Secularity God
Major Movements	Jewish-Christianity Gnosticism Scriptures	Worship Canon Creeds Office Councils	Biblical Interpretation Scholasticism Crusades Inquisitions	Humanism *Devotio Moderna* Conciliarism Reformation	Scientific Method Enlightenment Catholic Revival	Rationalism Liberal Theologies Neo-Scholasticism	Vatican Council II Religious Freedom Theologies of Liberation
Major Prophets, Traditionists, and Visionaries	Justin Martyr Irenaeus *The Shepherd of Hermas*	Augustine Benedict	Gregory VII Thomas Aquinas Francis of Assisi	Luther, Zwingli, Calvin; Trent, Jesuits, Bellarmine	Jansen, Pascal, Galileo; Manualist Theologies	Drey Newman Kleutgen Leo XIII	John XXIII Guttierez Lonergan Rahner Schillebeeckx
Permanent Exigencies	Symbolic	Communitarian Interpretive	Systematic Theoretic	Dialectical Critical	Methodological	Transcendental	Communicative
Emergent Fields of Theology		Trinity Christology	Sacraments Ethics Soteriology	Anthropology Grace	Ecclesiology Dogmatics Moral Theology Missiology	Philosophy of Religion Revelation and Faith Eschatology	Religious Education Pastoral Studies Comparative Religion

story of Jesus must be interiorized, but also that the will to understand is always a gift.

The probing attempts (5) to face modern and contemporary pluralistic cultures over the past three hundred years have not always been successful. Some Catholics have wanted to jettison the past to travel lightly; others have wanted to package each item without wondering whether some past baggage is worth carrying. But the contemporary world of scientific method, critical self-understanding, and historical self-making (6) refuses to disappear. They continue to ask whether it is possible to respeak the images, symbols, and stories, to reinterpret the conflicting understandings, to resocialize the doctrinal structural norms, and to rethink the theological discipline as a respected voice among contemporary claimants for the construction of our world (7). More importantly, our world continues to ask whether these reinterpretations will be more than merely human words, whether they can be what they claim to be—Divine words whose consoling, reconciling force may be reexperienced, freshly disclosed, and newly understood.

This movement we have sketched over some nineteen hundred years is not due simply to external forces pushing against the Christian community. For it has sometimes been said that the doctrines of the early Church, like that of the Triune God proclaimed at Nicaea (325 C.E.), were only defined because someone denied them. But in fact the energy of the Gospel itself as it encountered new cultural horizons invited the developments.

What we think of now as specifically Catholic aspects of Christian history, such as Scholasticism, medieval Christendom, or baroque art emerged from questions, interpretations, and judgments made by believers over the centuries as a response to the Gospel. Medieval theories about salvation arose due to issues raised by the Pauline images of ransom, adoption, and sacrifice. Systems were necessary simply to coordinate the various doctrines of the community. And Christian governments of one sort or another keep emerging because the call of Christ was not simply to fishermen in Galilee, but to all men and women. As Catholic history developed, it encountered new forms of life which it constantly attempted to understand and transform.

The characteristic Catholic past remains part of the present duties of the community. Although our symbols, institutional interpretations, theories, and practice cannot repeat that past, they will echo it in new ways. The focus of unity for Catholics will remain the same: sacramental life, the official leadership of bishops and pope, and the prophets and visionaries who hover at our peripheral sightlines, forbidding compromise with evil and challenging believers toward heroic charity. The Catholic Church sees itself as an *ecclesia semper reformanda,* an assembly always (in need of) reforming itself according to the call of the Gospel and the human situation.

A NARROW VISION?

Is this a tunnel vision of the world? Is it some fixation on a pristine point of the past which seems intrinsically more perfect than our present? Hardly.

Catholicism has a fundamentally universal outreach. This evangelical program is not abstract, a merely vague intention to offer warm comfort to millions. Rather it is a universal call which is reached by sharp interest paid to its own particular Tradition and to the local situation in which it finds itself. The Catholic trust in the underlying "stuff" of its own history is a conviction that its very specificity has ultimate significance. The believer gives a cup of water to one "little one," because in that single human face the All discloses its love.

Yet even this formulation is too abstract. Catholicism's difficult work into the next millennium will require listening to, thinking through, and acting upon the common cultural experiences of our planet: the growth of secularized humanity; consumerist economics; bureaucratization of both capitalist and socialist economies; and the reactionary attitudes of fundamentalist religious, national, and racial movements.

If the spiritual meaning of humanity is to be proclaimed to these concrete problems, then intercultural, interreligious, and transnational dialogues must occur. The global humanity that is emerging from the confusions of this century will demand an authentic hearing from believers so that the true universality of the Gospel may be preached.

This task—plunging into the particularities of our own Tradition and the human situations of those to whom we speak—will also be accomplished under a new and difficult state of Diaspora. This dispersal of believers among the culturally disinterested will not be unlike the experience of the Hellenistic world at the beginning of our common era. In this, Christians will have much to learn from their Jewish brothers and sisters who have suffered the isolation of surrounding social structures and the difficulties of maintaining belief and practice under the persecution for religious values held up to an indifferent world. For with their Lord, Christians have little reason to assure themselves that earthly success will be theirs. Smaller Christian communities, less economically established, again prophetically visible, may be called upon to preach the Gospel to increasingly hostile societies.

DOES CATHOLICISM HAVE A CONCRETE PROGRAM FOR THE FUTURE?

Some people, even Catholics themselves, think that there is a blueprint for the Christian future of the world. Some place this treasured program in a literal or allegorical reading of the Scriptures, especially the Book of Revelation; some put it in the Pope or in some message locked away in the Vatican library's vaults. But in fact, any such printout of the future would be a misunderstanding of the Christian message—and more importantly, of the Christian God.

The God we worship is not a God who discloses the day and hour of the divine will for our world; indeed, it is hidden in the Cross and Resurrection of Jesus Christ. Catholic Christians have no special access to a computerized version of the crystal ball. In fact, they must trust in God's presence and promises in the past, their loving interpretation of that past in the present, and their discerning hope for God's Grace in their future. Catholics react to contemporary events with the measure of intelligence, wit, and grace granted them by faith, hope, and love. The tools available to them remain the stories of the Gospel and Tradition, the interpretations of the prophets and teachers of the past, the theories and systems which collected the truth and anticipated the precarious present.

Now Catholics are most likely to be found at the edges of moral and religious issues in our societies: problems of life and death—abortion, war, health care for the handicapped or senile, security for the poor and disenfranchised; problems of the quality of life—working conditions, just wages, education, family life, marriage, and divorce; and sociocultural and economic planning—political campaigns, think tanks, nuclear disarmament, and diplomacy. These public questions have become the crucible in which Catholic (or rather global) identity will be formed.

In the disintegration of the classical certitudes of society, Catholics have become conscious with others that virtue cannot be merely a private affair. Patience, courage, prudence, justice, and temperance are not primarily intra-Christian matters, but must wend their way into the larger world. In this sense, Catholics expect their institution as it embodies the Good News to proclaim, confront, and transform social structures with the same vigor and creativity that it met Semitic, Greco-Roman, Celtic, Germanic, Slavic, and New World cultures.

For the self-making of humanity since the Enlightenment has not been an unalloyed success by anyone's measure, let alone a Divine standard. What was once a series of national warring states has become a world in search of organic unity in which power must be guided not by opportunism but by wisdom. With the possibility of destroying whole regions of the earth, even entire populations, through nuclear self-destruction, no single individual, no government can afford to be less than globally conscious—even if it is only searching for some place to preserve its own survival.

The unthinkable holocausts of this century have given rise to the equally unthinkable possibilities of "life" after nuclear war. We can resign ourselves either to the long cycle of human decline, narrowing our experience to self-interest, impoverishing our understandings of the world through heart-felt blindness, tunneling our judgments into self-protective bunkers, and fencing our values with fear; or, facing our disenchantment with the technocratic elite, we can collaborate toward a new society.

Achieving a new, federated, pluralistic, global social order will be difficult, entailing suffering for the "haves" as well as the "have-nots." And none of us likes pain. So we establish elaborate defense mechanisms to protect ourselves from deprivation, hoping that we can stave off the nihilism which threatens destruction.

In this mixed world, compromised between authentic values of development and despair, the Catholic community offers the Gospel of Jesus. It proclaims a community *within* suffering, not an escape from it. It combines individuals into a loving family of faithful, hopeful agents whose lives contribute to the liberation of the most authentic social and personal impulses. In any societal transformation, in any transculturation of Gospel values, martyrs appear— whether the bloody witnesses to liberation in Middle and South America or Asia, or the confessing dissenters in developed countries whose work, actions, and persons are isolated, muted, and sometimes lost in silence.

Catholic prophets are supported by their institution when Pope Paul VI speaks to the United Nations and cries: "No more war, war never again!" The institutional vision is instanced when small basic communities of Catholics take the Eucharistic readings, pray over them, and apply them to their personal, familial, and working lives. The society is judged by Catholic visionaries when men and women march upon governmental assemblies in support of human life. Catholics, rather than dealing some prepackaged deck of cards to a less-than-waiting world, search for the *legitimate means* of societal and personal transformation that will allow a new earth to be granted by God. The harsh work of disclosing the Gospel *within* the world and of confronting the world *with* the Gospel is at the heart of Catholic sensibilities and understanding in this century.

Thus Catholics and their pastors have begun to be a people on the margins, individuals caught between the social bodies of world policy. They hope to become a place of dialogue in which reconciliation may occur—a situation of centering in which transcendence may again appear. They recognize that the world cannot envision itself anew unless they themselves enact the transformation they expect of society. Their compassion for one another will be their suffering with the change of society itself. As they interrelate rich and poor people and nations, primitive and scientific societies, they hope to become a unified narrative voice on behalf of authentic humanity.

Every social institution at present pretends to universal dominion: political ideologies—whether socialist or capitalist—supranational businesses, racial hegemonies, even religious polities. Catholicism cannot identify with any of these powers. To face the fact that despite its own historical temptations and sins, it is not an ideology—whether political, economic, racial, *or* religious—but a faith in God's future for the world requires a slip from the old cultural moorings and a self-conscious launch on its own evangelical mobility. That process is even now taking place.

There remain controversial ecclesiastical issues (mandatory celibacy for presbyters and bishops; sexual, marital, familial, and ethical conflicts; the ordination and roles of women; the authentic collegiality of authority; etc.) to be resolved. Even more important, there are external questions (such as war and peace or genetic engineering) to be undertaken. Each goes to the heart of the Gospel, each emerges from the vital organs of a struggling culture, each requires the difficult prospect of laying down one's life for one's friends.

But Catholics have never wanted for prophets, visionaries, or the authentic proponents of Tradition in the past. The contemporary versatility of Catholic internal conversation is vigorous; and if it has sometimes shown the sinfulness of men and women, it has also disclosed the heroic charity of saints and the glory of God. Jesus' declaration that he would never leave his Church untended ("I am with you always, even to the end of time"—Matt. 28:20, NEB) through the gift of his Spirit (John 14:15–17) has verified itself in the history of this people. Catholics have no reason to lose their trust that God will bless his Church with the individuals and movements necessary to conserve its past, challenge its present, and transform its future.

The modern meaning of Catholicism rests upon the command to preach the Good News. Catholics do not have reason for nostalgia or despair—but only for excitement at the tasks which await the apostolic community of believers. As Pope Paul VI said in his *Encyclical Letter on Evangelization:*

May the world of our time, which is searching, sometimes with anguish, sometimes with hope, be enabled to receive the Good News not from evangelizers who are dejected, discouraged, impatient or anxious, but ministers of the Gospel whose lives glow with fervor, who have first received the joy of Christ, and who are willing to risk their lives so that the Kingdom may be proclaimed and the Church established in the midst of the world.[4]

Now, of course, there are only hints and guesses, hints followed by guesses, as T. S. Eliot has said in his *Four Quartets*. But, in this matter of God's Kingdom, ours is only the trying, the attempts at achievement. The rest is not our business.

NOTES

1. Flannery O'Connor, *Habit of Being*, ed. Sally Fitzgerald (New York: Farrar, Straus & Giroux, 1979), 354.

2. Ibid., 477.

3. Pierre Teilhard de Chardin, "The Convergence of the Universe" (23 July 1951), in *Activation of Energy*, trans. René Hague (New York: Harcourt Brace Jovanovich, 1970), 294–95.

4. *Acta Apostolicae Sedis*, LXVIII (1976), par. 80, pp. 72–75. An English text may be found in *Evangelization Today*, ed. Austin Flannery (Northport, N.Y.: Costello, 1977), 48.

INDEX OF AUTHORS

INDEX OF SUBJECTS